Windows

Windows

A Prayer Journal

ANDREW M. GREELEY

CROSSROAD • NEW YORK

1995

The Crossroad Publishing Company
370 Lexington Avenue, New York, NY 10017

Copyright © 1995 by Andrew M. Greeley

Printed in the United States of America

Library of Congress Cataloging-in-Publication Data

Greeley, Andrew M., 1928–
    Windows : a prayer journal / Andrew M. Greeley
      p. cm.
    Sequel to: Sacraments of love and Love affair.
    ISBN 0-8245-1517-X (pbk.)
    1. Greeley, Andrew M., 1928—Diaries. 2. Catholic Church—United
States—Clergy—Diaries. 3. Spiritual journals. I. Title.
BX4705.G618A3 1995
248.3′2—dc20
                                            95-20307
                                                  CIP

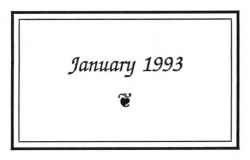

January 1993

January 29, 1993 — Tucson

My Love,

I woke up and can't go back to sleep. So I'll talk to You. The wise man, says the poem I read last night, tastes the Tigris in every sip. That means that in every bit of life there is a taste of the Whole, by which he means You. I believe that, though sometimes it's hard to imagine who or what the Whole is. Sometimes? That is to laugh! Always! Who are You? Why are You? What are You up to? If Love is what it's all about, if You are Love, how can it be that Love is? And why is it? And why am I?

Weird thoughts for this hour of the morning as I approach my sixty-fifth birthday, weird thoughts altogether. Yet the Arab poet is right. I taste You in everything, in the sip of water, in the ice tea, in the herbal tea, in the diet Coke, in the wonderful wine, in all the loves of my life, some of which are quite difficult these days.

I'm leaving tomorrow to go back to Chicago for my sixty-fifth birthday. Life slips through my fingers. I don't appreciate Your presence enough or Your gifts or Your love.

I don't savor the whole of Lake Michigan in a single sip. I am not aware enough of Your goodness and greatness lurking everywhere. Help me to be more aware. Help me to love You more. Help me on this weary night to grow old in such a way that I am light for others.

Help me to sleep now. I love You.

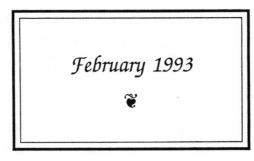

February 1993

February 3, 1993 — Chicago

My Love,

I want to reflect this morning on the little scene I watched at Little Company of Mary Hospital on Monday. I was walking with Dr. Marty Phee from the hospital cafeteria to his offices across the street. At the emergency door an elderly man was being unloaded from an ambulance. He was conscious and sitting up, but looked very sick. His wife was standing by his side, her thin face twisted in pain.

They were both well into their eighties and quite good looking, kind of distinguished. I suspect they must have married during the Great Depression or perhaps the War. Handsome young man, pretty wife, maybe the former in uniform. How much they must have seen together, how many joys and tragedies they must have shared together! Now time was running out on them — youth long gone, bodies weakening, dreams over, their lives near the end.

So it is with all of us, all the dreams and the hopes and plans dwindle down to an emergency room at the hospital.

The woman was not crying.

How should people like them look back on their lives?

With joy over its good times or sorrows over its failures and disappointments? Are the fading memories happy memories, are they anticipations of that which are yet to come?

Some would say it's all absurdity. I say that such persons as that couple are too important to be lost to You. They represent traces of the transcendent, as Hans Küng writes. You lurk everywhere. If each of them were sufficiently loveable to stay together in their marriage, it is because somehow they have become sacraments of Your love. If I hate to think about their lives being snuffed out, how much more would You who knows them and loves them intimately care for them? If You are a God who lives up to Your promises (which You surely are), You can't let love like theirs come to an end. If I felt sympathy for them, how much more would You feel for them?

William James began to believe in life after death because he could not accept that the bonds of love could be forever sundered. What that dear couple had and what they still have are an anticipation of love that is to come.

James is absolutely right. It would be intolerable for love to be permanently sundered. A universe that did that would not be a universe worth living in. And a God who permits people to be cheated of what their experiences of love seem to propound would not be a very good God at all. It certainly wouldn't be the God You claim to be.

So the ultimate issue is whether one can permit experiences of love to be revelatory or whether they are the ultimate in self-deception. Our fundamental instinct is that creation does make sense and that love can never end.

Take care of that couple and of all elderly couples and help them to trust in the goodness of Your plan.

February 5, 1993 — Chicago

My Love,

I'm sixty-five years and a few hours old. And I feel fine! For all the graces of these six and a half decades I am profoundly grateful, especially for the parents who made me what I am both biologically and religiously. I hope they are with You — also my Parent — rejoicing today. I am especially grateful for my health, which enables me to feel not old at all. I accept all that in Your plan awaits me and ask for the grace to make that acceptance cheerful and generous.

I like the notion that You are my Parent too and that every day is a birthday for many of Your children. I'm sure that like every parent You celebrate, though all the birthday parties must be a little bit boring, or they would be if You were capable of boredom. I intend the Mass and the party today to be eucharistic, thanksgiving for my family and my friends, a party in which I reward them generously (since I am able to do so) for their role in being Your graces for me. Help me to be cheerful and relaxed and not to get tired or irritable at the party — for which many folks worked very hard indeed.

Thank You, thank You, thank You, especially for the gift of life, the most precious gift of all and, as Chesterton put it, too important ever to be anything but life.

I Love You. Thank You for my life.

February 7, 1993 — Chicago

My Love,

What, I ask myself this morning, will I do with the rest of your life, now that I'm sixty-five? The answer, I think, is not much different from what I've done for the first sixty-five years. I'm not retiring, I'm not going to stop working, I'm not going to quiet down. I'm not going to in effect repudiate all that I've done by not doing it any more when I am perfectly capable healthwise of continuing to do it.

I do, however, intend to spend more time praying and reflecting. I know that You have heard me say that before and that it has been an empty promise. But I intend to keep trying and with more determination if not more success, since You are the only one that can grant success. But my return to Tucson tomorrow should be a good time to begin, especially since I do seem to be more mellow and more relaxed than I have been in a long time.

Again I want to thank You for all the great gifts of my life, especially for the blessings of family and friends.

And I love You.

February 9, 1993 — Tucson

My Love,

I continue to distract myself with the pleasure of my work, with my enthusiasms, my insights, my causes, my hopes, my plans, my angers. But what else is there to do? We will live while there is light and we trust in You, Your loving mercy as the psalm describes it, Your endless forgiveness, Your intimacy with us as illustrated by Jesus washing the feet of his followers.

Again what other way is there to go? Sure, life is vanity and chasing the wind, but while we live we have to chase the winds or die humanly long before our time.

So I thank You for the winds I have been able to chase and will continue to chase, and I love You.

February 12, 1993 — Tucson

My Love,

Qohelet in this morning's reading really takes on the Wisdom tradition. He has seen good and wise men suffer and foolish and evil men prosper. Therefore he can give no advice on how to live because everything in this world is vanity, absurdity, chasing after the wind. The only way to live is to fear You.

To some extent we dismiss Qohelet and his rantings because we have gone beyond him, or think we have. We think we have put aside the problem of evil or the mystery of life. We speak so facilely the religious formulae and clichés that respond to his problem. We cannot put ourselves into the position of a man who didn't even have these clichés but who knew that the clichés from the wisdom tradition were not enough. Qohelet has a good point to make, and I ought not dismiss him as a pain in the neck as I have done in the past. Life is mystery and to say that You are the mystery is true enough, but it doesn't end the mystery, does it?

The only leap we have made beyond Qohelet is to realize that You are not only mystery but Love and that, while we are well advised to live in fear of You, we must also go beyond fear to Love.

I certainly believe that — even when my sinus cough is driving me nuts. We are so limited by our physical bodies, it is so difficult to dialogue with the ineffable, even though I have come to believe that You are an intimate lover who has taken special care of me during my life.

Help me to keep loving You.

February 13, 1993 — Tucson

My Love,

Qohelet tells us this morning how hard it is to find a good woman, but he adds that it is also hard to find a good man. Then characteristically he says that it is all absurdity anyway. In effect he's saying that Your ways are mysterious, especially in the man/woman relationship. It is so much a sacrament of Your love and at the same time such an immense barrier to its own sacramentality. You have made the genders sufficiently different as to be attractive to one another and at the same time so different as to drive each other up the wall. Moreover the energies and dynamisms that are released at different times in the relationship are so powerful and so disconcerting — and so surprising — that the relationship often is in a state of near collapse. All things considered, it is marvelous that all of them don't end, especially now that they are not cut short in a decade or so by the death of one or the other partner.

Yet love is stronger than death and even more so is Love. I think from my perspective on the outside that I understand a little of its tensions and rewards, but just enough to know that I am not an expert and neither is anyone else.

Maybe it is a sacrament of our relationship with You, which is so often troubled but which is also stronger than death.

I love You.

February 18, 1993 — Tucson

My Love,

The president's state of the union speech last night with its elaborate economic plans was courageous. Whether he will get it through and whether it will help or hurt the country remains to be seen. Qohelet would of course call it folly, chasing the wind, but then he thinks all human behavior is folly. We social scientists would call it the problem of unanticipated consequences or even more obscurely latent dysfunctions. A better name might be Murphy's law — if things can go bad they will. Or as the late Gus Weigel (Be good to him) said of the Council all human enterprises, given sufficient time, go badly.

Qohelet's theory is that when that happens it is part of Your plan. You have different goals than do the people that make the plans. Since they don't know what You're up to, their programs tend to fail. Well, that's putting Qohelet into modern terms, but that's what he means. The president in other words is taking a big risk because so many things can go wrong.

So it is with all our plans and projects. A lot of things can go wrong. Sometimes in my own life when things have gone wrong I can see Your hand in them directing the trajectory of my life — as I look back on them. Other times the things that go wrong seem to be the result of merely the random accidents of life. That gets me once again into the endlessly baffling question of Your providence — to which none of my theologian friends can give a satisfying answer.

And here is where Qohelet, again translated into modern terms, becomes valuable. Since we don't know what You're up to but we do know that You love us, we must "go with the flow" and trust in that love whenever things go wrong. And we must not be afraid to take risks when they're necessary because we rest, as the Irish saying goes, in the palm of Your hand.

In which place I again say that I love You — even if I don't understand what You're up to.

February 21, 1993 — Tucson

My Love,

Last night I went to see *The Cemetery Club*. I was interested to see how they handled the theme of love between older people. It was a terrible film. I almost walked out. It mixed vulgar laughter at death and aging, at the expense of older people, with cheap sentimentality and an occasional moment of sensitive tenderness. To make matters worse the audience was especially loud and vulgar and its laughter just a little sick.

Maybe I was in a bad mood!

It was an interesting contrast with my data analysis of belief in life after death, and especially the interesting finding that in former socialist countries belief in survival is higher among the young than it is among those who are immediately older than them. A revival of religion? Or maybe only a revival of hope?

There wasn't much hope in the film or much faith or much love for that matter. Death is not funny, older people are not funny, love between those over fifty is not funny, survival is not funny, and melancholy visits to a cemetery are not funny. Only the sick and the vulgar think they are.

Anyway, thanks to Your gift of faith, I believe that death does not say the final word and that life is too important to be anything but life. Is there any escape from vulgarity and sentimentality when you don't have hope?

Help me, my Love, to have hope and to continue to have it.

I love You.

February 26, 1993 — Tucson

My Love,

Two small tragedies in the news yesterday: a twenty-three-year-old Irish nurse killed by gunfire in Somalia. A two-year-old-girl killed by a bomb in Sarajevo. Two lives needlessly blotted out by evil people before they had a chance to begin. I knew neither of them obviously. Yet I mourn for them. You who loved them with a mother's love must mourn them with great grief. I must believe that You will wipe away the tears and renew their lives. Do I have to believe that You will punish the killers? You love them too. I don't understand how You operate in these matters and it is not necessary that I understand. But there is profound evil in the world and good just barely survives in the face of it. I don't understand. I do know that You are love and there's nothing to be gained by trying to second guess You. I must do my part, such as it is, and leave the rest in Your hands.

But I don't understand.

I do, however, continue to love You, however poorly.

February 27, 1993 — Tucson

My Love,

I've been reading medieval social history books lately as part of my work in the sociology of religion and am astonished at the extent and power of the belief in magic. The people of those eras were animists, believing in spirits with whom one could and indeed had to make deals. My own data show that a lot of their superstitions persist even into the present. Their purpose is to lower anxiety in a problematic and uncertain world, to reassure those who live in terror.

The psalm this morning says You made us a little less than the angels. But I doubt that there is so much anxiety among the angels. There is perhaps less anxiety today because we have medical cures for lots of ailments that our ancestors lacked. Yet anxiety persists because of the uncertainty and fragility of human life. So we try to make a deal with some of the powers that govern the universe; and we often do so by using Catholic doctrines and practices in quasi-magical fashion. We don't like being limited to a God who will not deal, a God who is not subject to our control, a God who plays Her own game and refuses to be manipulated by our incantations and such like, the kind of God Qohelet wrote about.

Magic seemed to work. Of course it really didn't work but at lest it provided temporary reassurance. There is nothing like that in our interactions with You. No deals, no temporary reassurance, no negotiations. Only love. Which is wonderful and beautiful and surprising.

You promise permanent reassurance in the long run but in the short run refuse to protect us from the powers of the lower air (such as the maniacs who set off the bomb in the World Trade Center yesterday). You want us to be Your children indeed but adult children. It is so hard to be an adult.

Anyway, I think I left behind long ago any trace of the Catholic magic and have become profoundly skeptical about all claims to the miraculous. Not that I doubt Your power to interfere, but only that You do so routinely. I don't think my skepticism has destroyed my capacity for wonder. I hope not. Keep it alive in me, please.

And I love You.

March 1, 1993 — Tucson

My Love,

The selection this morning in the book of religious poems I'm reading is Hopkins's "God's Grandeur." The image of Your spirit "brooding over the world with warm breast and, ah! bright wings" is almost a cliché, I've heard it so often. Yet what a lovely image! It conveys better than almost any other metaphor the explosion of goodness in Your creation — a goodness that reflects You and Your love.

Hate-filled images scream out in this morning's paper: gun fights in Texas, bombs exploding all over the world, violent battles with "fundamentalists" — human ugliness defacing Your grandeur.

What to make of it all! So much good, so much evil. Why don't we see the grandeur Hopkins demands?

There is just so much uselessness, especially now in the matter of sexual abuse of children. On this rainy and cold Monday morning with my sinuses blocked and a busy crazy day ahead of me I am depressed by the ugliness and not as reassured as I should be by either the grandeur or Jesus' promise. I still love You and always will but just now I'm afraid I don't feel much like looking for the Spirit hovering above things.

And I wouldn't be able to see Her anyway because of the rain clouds!

March 4, 1993 — Tucson

My Love,

This morning I read Hopkins's poem in which he thanks You for dappled things, like "couple-colored" skies. Or the dappled half moon that hung over my garden last night. The moon is only an extra large rock that drifted into the earth's orbit a long time ago and helps to keep the latter stable. Yet how much it has meant and still means to lovers, and how romantic it is hanging up there in the sky. It's a minor phenomenon in the cosmos, something that causes You no effort, yet it means so much to us — like so many other things in Your dappled creation. Thank You.

March 5, 1993 — Tucson

My Love,

I read from Rabbi Gene Borowtiz's book on the way to San Antonio and back and was impressed. We live, he writes, in gratitude, even for life itself and all the other gifts. This finally is the only answer we have to evil and ugliness.

I was awash in gratitude in San Antonio last night. Once again it was absolutely clear that my novels have a tremendous positive impact on people's live — the Presbyterian minister who said he head learned more about God's love from the stories than he had in all his years in a Presbyterian seminary. And there were so many others.

Despite all the struggles, the books are worth writing and I should never permit myself to get discouraged. Rather I should walk in a sea of gratitude for Your blessing me with the opportunity to tell such stories.

I do thank You and I do love You.

March 8, 1993 — Tucson

My Love,

The moon was out there again last night, grinning from dusk to dawn as she bathed the earth in silver. Our little blue planet with its white satellite doesn't matter much in the cosmic scale of things, yet they can put on a show that dazzles those "immortal diamonds" (as Hopkins calls us) who inhabit the earth.

Do You admire the full white moon in the clear night sky? I'm sure You do. It may be a minor feat in Your repertoire of wonderful tricks, but You doubtless enjoy even the small tricks and enjoy even more our delight, because in the case of the desert moon there are observers to share in Your enjoyment.

So even in a "demythologized" cosmos, it is fair to see the moon as part of Your splendor and indeed a splendor arrayed and displayed for us. For which splendor I am grateful and in response to which again I tell You that I love You.

March 9, 1993 — Tucson

My Love,

I had supper with some old friends from Chicago last night, a happy couple in their own love but with great tragedies in their family. I admire their courage and their faith. In many ways my own life is so much easier. The celibate may have to worry about all the people he has tried to help and failed but they're not his own flesh and blood. Despite all the crises and all my activities, I have not had a difficult life compared to this dear couple and to so many others I know. If the celibate life frees us for service, then we must ask how *well* we serve. How well do I serve?

I love You. Help me to love and serve You more, You who are the life and light of every "immortal diamond."

March 10, 1993 — Tucson

My Love,

The scandal in Santa Fe broke in the paper this morning, merely the facts about the archbishop's three women, not yet the rumor whether it was a ring of gays in the chancery who set him up. What a mess and what a disgrace to the Church. Ugly and profoundly disgusting.

If only they had taken steps a half decade ago to clean up the pedophile/gay mess in the chanceries. But they didn't, and now the whole Church is embarrassed and the priesthood is injured again, not that any of this will make any difference to the systematic denial of the problem by priests.

I began warning about these problems seven years ago. I don't feel good about my predictions being confirmed. I'd have been much happier if they had not been confirmed. But the problem is out in the open now. I hope finally some of the leaders wake up, but I fear that nothing will be accomplished. It will be once more a case of "too little, and too late." Not much left for me to do.

I'm off to Sedona for a day. Take care of us on the trip. I love You.

March 11, 1993 — Tucson

My Love,

The Cubs game went to eleven innings — they lost, of course — though I must say I took pride in strolling into El Charro with my Cubs cap on! I'm too tired for anything else. I'll be back tomorrow. I love You.

March 12, 1993 — Tucson

My Love,

A gigantic pine tree stands in front of my house. He is stately, calm, regal — surveying the events around him with aloof dignity and a certain amount of amused skepticism. He reminds me of my friend the moon, which was hiding behind clouds this morning like she had lost interest in earth and had turned away.

Science tells us that the tree is the result of a long evolutionary process and chance combination of elements. Nothing miraculous, nothing that reveals design in the universe. Once we get the single force theory we will know Your mind and all mystery will be swept away from the tree, as most of it has been from the moon. No room for poetry, for the solid majesty of the tree as a revelation of You and Your presence in the world. Wrong!

To explain the process doesn't explain the why. The tree is grace. It doesn't have to be there, but it is. The earth doesn't have to be here either but it is. Even the Cubs didn't have to come to Tucson last year but they did. Grace abounds. Sacraments are not explained away by scientific explanations, but are only made more profound. The single force still can't explain the why of anything. Once we go to why, we go to You.

You whom I love and will try always to love.

March 13, 1993 — Tucson

My Love,

I continue to ponder the mysteries of my life, the astonishing opportunities You have given me and the amazing
graces with which You have overwhelmed me. I thank You
for all of them, especially the most surprising ones. Why
You have treated me this way I do not know. I cannot
even begin to comprehend, but I am very grateful indeed. I
have no reason to complain about the things that have not
worked out so well. I must revel even more than I do in
the blessings and surprises.

The sexual abuse problem grows worse as the wind
that the Church has been sowing for so many years now
becomes the whirlwind that comes back for us to reap. Yet
the denial continues. Will it ever stop? I'm going to be
in the midst of that whirlwind the next couple of weeks
because, as it turns out, my new book will be published
right in the midst of the terrible, sordid crisis in Santa Fe.
I must keep by temper and my courage up during these
weeks. The latter isn't very hard because I'm so angry at
Church leaders and at so many of my fellow priests. When,
I wonder, will it ever end?

I love You.

March 15, 1993 — Tucson

My Love,

Here in Tucson with the weather in the eighties every
day (for which many, many thanks) it is hard to comprehend the fury of the snowstorm that swept the East Coast
this week — the worst storm of the century or at least of
the last half century. Hundreds killed, many more than in
the hurricanes the last couple of years. Just a few minutes

ago there was news of a freighter sunk during the storm with thirty-one crew aboard. Such terrible fury. Nature in a different form than my smiling moon or stately pine tree.

Are You present in the storm? In some sense You surely are, perhaps saving people who otherwise would have died.

And what of the war crimes trial of the Serbian soldier who raped and then killed nine women? One of them, his favorite, he killed with a machine gun.

Are You present in that rage and hatred? Again in some sense You must be, suffering with those nine women and now perhaps suffering with their killer.

What to make of all of this horror in the daily news stories?

I don't know what to make of it, except to sense the horror. It is so apparent. Will it ever end? I get a headache even trying to think about it.

Something like the headache I had last night because I had rushed too much during the past week. I'm sorry for that. I'm sorry that I let it interfere with my being the kind of host I should have been. I did pretty well, but not well enough, I fear.

Only fifteen more days here, and four of them in the East on my book promotion tour. It has all gone by much too quickly. I am grateful for the time here, however, and the work I've accomplished. I should have relaxed more — how often have I said that — and now it's too late.

Will I ever learn? I love You.

March 16, 1993 — Tucson

My Love,

I had supper last night with a Chicago priest who had been driven out of his parish a number of years ago by one of the worst of the pedophile predators. He has lost his parents, his only brother, and his aunt and uncle in the last few years as well as his parish. He's a kind and gentle soul who has been battered savagely and still is kind and gentle. I felt sorry for him but also respected his courage. How different my life is, harried and hassled by all the work I have to do this week while this good man waits for weekend assignments from the Tucson chancery.

However hassled, I love You, thank You.

March 17, 1993, St. Patrick's Day — Tucson

My Love,

When I'm as dull and worn on Paddy's day as I am now there is something terrible wrong with my life. I read Eileen Durkin's wonderful little play for Old St. Patrick's today and was deeply moved by it and by the wonderful story of the Irish and the faith. But I'm too numb, yes, that's a good word, numb to do much with it.

I'm sorry to dump all this on You. I'll turn on some Irish music now. Maybe it will change my mood.

Help me, my Love, I beg You.

March 19, 1993 — Tucson

My Love,

The interviewer from *Modern Maturity* came yesterday. He was a nice man, and mostly interested in quotes from my non-fiction books.

But the quotes revealed to me again what a crazy life I have been living all these years, how much I have written on how many problems. He asked whether the silence in our family home during the tragedy of the Great Depression is responsible for my outpouring of words. Perhaps there's an insight there. More likely the reason is that I'm glib and free and blessed with my father's sense of justice and integrity.

So I have no reason to complain as the phone rings while I try to finish this important sociology project. It goes with the territory I have freely chosen, even if I didn't realize that when I chose the territory.

I ask again that the new book flourish, both because of its message and because of the need to revive the audience. Thank You for Your love, which I return as best I can.

March 20, 1993 — Tucson

My Love,

The Sanchez resignation and accompanying scandal is a terrible blow, one of many because of the pedophile thing, but a big one just the same. We priests are destroying the priesthood and no one seems to care.

And I work very hard all the time with little to show for my efforts.

Now isn't that a stupid statement! I'm sorry.

I guess I'm in one of my black Saturday moods, tired from the work and dreading next week.

I admit I have become obsessed by the sexual abuse of children by priests. It's high on my agenda, and it is an ugly subject. Terribly depressing, but I cannot and will not turn away from it. Too many children have suffered too much. On the other hand I must not let myself become shrill, either in my own head or in public.

Random and confused thoughts on a random and confused day. I feel so rushed, so hassled.

Yet I still love You as best I can.

March 21, 1993 — Tucson

My Love,

I still have the feeling that I'm running on empty, not a good way to begin a trip to New York and Washington. The latest effrontery from Rome is that the Signatura has ordered the bishop of Pittsburgh to reassign to a parish a priest accused of sexual abuse of children. This could lead to a rash of such decisions. They really don't care over there, in great part I suspect because pederasty is so common in the Italian church that no one thinks it's really wrong.

In the Gospel I will read in an hour or so over at Our Mother of Sorrows we will hear the story of the man born blind, another one of St. John's marvelously told tales. The center of it is when the man expresses total commitment to You through Jesus. That's what our lives are supposed to be about — no matter what happens and no matter how tired one feels. I think I am going to need a lot of that faith in the coming week.

I am so desperately worn out — and so discouraged by the pedophile mess. Please help me.

I love You.

March 24, 1993 — On the shuttle between New York and Washington...

My Love,

The day has gone well enough. *Good Morning America* was fine, the two press interviews went well, and Donahue was no worse than usual, though he is still a domineering demagogue. He interjected himself into the program and got in the way of what Jason Berry and I had to say and, worse, what the survivors of clergy abuse had to say.

Their stories were very moving, poor people. Most of them remain in the Church despite terrible things that have been done to them. It's one thing to support their cause, as I do, as a cause in justice and charity and it's quite another to hear them talk with anguish and terror about what some monster in a Roman collar has done to them. And still the Church continues to deny, stonewall, prevaricate. It's as terrible as ever, I'm afraid.

These poor people think I'm a hero because I've stood up for them. I'm not. There's no cost in it for me except the contempt of my fellow priests, and I had that anyway. I'm afraid the Church isn't going to do anything about the problem. It will just get worse and worse and worse. And the image of the priesthood will suffer more and more.

We're approaching Washington now. Thank You for all the opportunities You have given me. I love You.

March 25, 1993 — Tucson

My Love,

I bumped into the Cardinal [Bernardin] flying back from Washington, and we talked all the way. It would seem that the bishops are coming around on the pedophile thing, fairly dramatically in some sense, and beginning to buy his wise approach. The new review board had its first case the day before yesterday and it seemed to have worked well. Yet the Northbrook case continues to be an enormous barrier to his credibility with the press and the survivors. They must deal with it but they don't seem to know how. Please take good care of the Cardinal.

The tour has been a success, though whether it will save the book or not remains to be seen. We'll know by the end of next week.

I thank You for the success of the trip and for granting me the quickness to respond to so many questions.

And I love You.

March 29, 1993 — Tucson

My Love,

Someone remarked at supper the other night that they had read a sign at a protest (probably a "Christian" one) that began, "God hates...." She said she turned away from the sign because she knew that You didn't hate.

Yet the image of the vengeful, punitive God persists, doesn't it? Thus in the psalm I read today You are pictured as knocking enemies around and slaughtering them. We are all so eager to get You on our side so that You will dispose of said enemies. In the process we forget about all the things You have said about Yourself and Your son Jesus has said about You.

In the book by Barnardt that Tom McCormack gave me You are presented as whispering to characters — in Your maternal, Spirit mode. It is a real *tour de force* as novel technique.

More interestingly his God is very like You. I wonder if there is a necessity of portraying You that way when You have a walk-on role. It's the same God as appears in the films (*The Rapture* excepted). Maybe Your presence and Your image are so strong that when You're on stage we must present You the way You are.

How, I wonder, did I come to know You that way. Maybe through the Lady Wisdom in Roland's article and then giving You a part in my autobiography. And then I knew You through some of the women in my life too — indeed knew You as vulnerable. But it was in the autobiography that I discovered You and came to love You the way I should. No, to *begin* to love You the way I should. I have so much more to learn about You and how I should love You.

Maybe I should bring You even more into one of my novels.

March 30, 1993 — Tucson

My Love,

Last full day in Tucson. Again many thanks for this part of my life.

I've been giving interviews at a rapid clip. It's a strange sort of thing. I did not write the book so that it would appear at a time of crisis on the pedophile scandal. Nor was the publication date set to correspond with an anticipated crisis. Moreover, it is good for the Church that at least one priest is in the media supporting victims and demanding changes and explaining the problem. But at the same time I'm plugging the book. How do I keep all the motives straight in a situation like this? As I look over the interviews I think I've done it right — I'm truthful, I don't go to extremes, my anger shows. And of course I mention the book, which is what an author should do. Rarely have my multiple roles been in conflict, but this time there is, if not a conflict, at least an uneasiness. Help me to continue to do it right.

We'll know by tomorrow whether the book will fly or not. It seems strange that only a week after publication date a book's fate is decided. Again I ask You that it be a success for reasons You understand, which are not basically my personal reasons at all (or at least not much).

The Haunted Book Store near here sold out on Friday and now has a waiting list. They know pretty well how many books they usually sell, so that's a good sign, especially since the book did not get as much publicity here as it did elsewhere.

I often wonder how I ever got into a situation in which I worry about something like this.

The wild flowers are so lovely this year — fairy dust, desert marigolds. I don't have much time for them or for my friend Moon, who is turning her face toward us again (and through my curtains last night). She's grinning because she knows that when she's full next week she signals the coming of Easter and Passover.

I love You and I thank You again for my Tucson experience.

March 31, 1993 — En Route from Tucson to Chicago

My Love,

Eighty degrees in Tucson and sunny. Thirty-five in Chicago and rain, with snow possible tonight. Yet I am glad to be going home, though the goodbyes were painful. I had supper at [University of Arizona] President Pacheco's last night. Charming people and real fans of my novels. They like me, which is always a nice experience. For that many thanks.

Leaving is always a mad rush. I was exhausted by the time I got to the airport. And I face the usual transition hassle when I get back, with perhaps more demands than usual. I have to learn how to say no firmly to people who want to eat into the little time I have.

I won't do that of course. Priests must not do that.

I visited Bishop Green at the Holy Family Center — old people's home. He was in great spirits, happy at the good life he has lived. But the place for all its brightness and smiling staff is gloomy. There are so many wretchedly unhappy men and women in it. Growing old is not easy. The body and the mind deteriorate. The person returns to infancy, sometimes as dependent as a baby. It happens to all of us, and it will happen to me.

Well, You know best and I accept whatever You have in store for me. I have the sense, to tell You the truth, that I am stretching the rubber band a little thin, trying to do ever more in life with somewhat less energy. This transition departure from Tucson was the worst yet. I don't think I've ever been so exhausted on the trip back.

Anyway I love You and thanks for both the time in Tucson and for bringing me home—and for such a wonderful home to come home to: Chicago!

April 1993

April 1, 1993 — Chicago

My Love,

Back to an April 1 blizzard and chaos in the apartment. I hope to have it cleaned up by the end of the day. Class begins. Rush, rush, rush.

I love You.

P.S. Someone wrote a nasty letter about the first volume of this journal [*Love Affair*]. I had no cause for complaint, he said, because I had chosen the life I find myself in. I don't think he understands the nature of love. One unburdens oneself to the beloved regardless of whether the problems are the result of free choice. Oh, well, I will continue to share everything with You.

April 4, 1993 — Chicago

My Love,

I watched *Green Pastures* last night. It was a very old film, the acting left something to be desired, and I suppose some of it might be written off today as racial, not to say racist, stereotyping. Nonetheless it was a perfect beginning for the Holy Week themes. The conclusion of the film is that God became merciful only when He (Rex Ingram) learned how to suffer. I think we would rephrase it a bit and say that we discovered Your mercy only when we realized that You suffered, and suffer with us, and that Good Friday is the revelation of that suffering. As I told the people at Mass yesterday afternoon: this is the week that we celebrate the fact that we will not die alone, that You have already, as best as God can, walked the valley of death and will do so again when each of Your beloved creatures dies.

Moreover, just as we die with You, so we will rise with You. There can be no more encouraging truths: we do not die alone, and we will rise again!

It's a hard truth to believe because death seems so final. But we know in our heart that it is not final. Jesus, Good Friday, Easter — all are ways of telling us that what we suspect and hope for and long for in our hearts is indeed true.

That gives me a lot to hope for this busy and Holy Week. So hope I will, with Your help.

Leo wrote a strong letter in my defense in the parish paper yesterday. A friend when You really need a friend. For that too I am grateful.

And I love You, my best friend of all.

March 8, 1993, Holy Thursday — Chicago

My Love,

Today is the alleged anniversary of the founding of the priesthood. Leaving aside the question of whether it is an anachronism to read back the priesthood as we now know it to the final meals of Jesus and his apostles, it is as good a time as any, and better than most, to consider priestly commitments. Mine are as strong as ever, as strong as they were in second grade, eighth grade, ordination day, silver jubilee. For which grace many thanks to You. But this year I have less regard for the priesthood, not as a state, not as sacrament, but as a collectivity than, I ever had had before. The failure of my fellow priests to assume responsibility for the sexual abuse crisis, the soft thinking about the value of celibacy, the insensitivity to the laity — all of these are a disgrace and more than a disgrace; they are astonishingly self-destructive. I find that when I'm talking about this on the various interviews for the new book that my voice rises and my throat tightens. What so many priests are doing today infuriates me. They are destroying, heedlessly, needlessly, all that was good in the priesthood into which we were ordained. It is absolute folly.

Moreover they will renew their pledges tonight with serene self-confidence and righteousness.

Well, the original twelve were not all that great shakes either, were they?

And neither am I as far as that goes. If I see the issues today a bit more clearly, the reason is that I have been blessed with special opportunities and special graces.

Yet today I want to pray for the priesthood, tarnished and tattered as it is, that it will become more what You want it to be.

April 9, 1993, Good Friday — Chicago

My Love,

The liturgy at St. Mary of the Woods was marvelous. Today the teenagers did a passion play that was perfect, and last night we washed the hands of everyone in the church. In both cases it was very much a family sort of event that the people clearly felt part of. Creative liturgy at its most intelligent and tasteful.

You know all of this of course, but one talks about such things with a Lover. Both liturgies put me in a Holy Week frame of mind, which is what liturgy is supposed to do.

The bottom line is that Good Friday is where Love, that is, You, went as far as You could possibly go to reveal the depth and the passion of that Love.

You are a God who loves beyond the possibility of human comprehension. It is so clear this week that it is difficult to miss the truth. But we sure have obscured it for a long time. Even now when we preach it as best we can, some of the laity grow uneasy. "Our salvation is assured," we say in the liturgy today. How much that runs against what was taught in school or catechism for so long. We made You a God of wrath instead of a God of mercy and love despite the prima facie evidence that You are not wrathful at all.

Well, I'm harried — phone just rang again — and exhausted, but I will try to reflect again tomorrow on the wondrous if evident and oft-repeated truth that You really are Love.

April 11, 1993, Easter Sunday — Chicago

My Love,

A little earlier the day seemed like those days when I was a child and feared the end of the world was at hand — dark, low clouds, thunder and lightning, pervasive gloom. Now it has lightened up a bit, but it's still not a day for Easter parades. However, the Easter that is inside us is what counts — though the sun helps too.

How much debate has there been about the events that we celebrate today! Did Jesus really rise? Would the phenomenon be captured on a videotape? Did the apostles merely believe that he was alive and this faith made him seem alive? Or, independent of belief, did he *really* rise? And was this a physical resurrection and not just a "spiritual" resurrection?

Again I wonder why there is this compulsion to admit the possibility of the marvelous but then limit the extent of the marvels?

Were Sinai and Easter merely natural events that we have made sacred or were they one of those times (rare or frequent) when You did intervene in the course of human events, setting aside, in some fashion, the laws of nature?

Once one admits that You started creation with the Big Bang, what is the point in trying to put limits on what You can do? That's always baffled me. As You know I am very skeptical of claims about the miraculous. (There are reports that the Mother of Jesus will appear in a Minnesota field today. I'm sure she has better things to do.) Nonetheless I see no reason for denying in principle Your power to intervene when You choose to. What's the point in being God if You can't do that?

But I'm sure that the question is wrongly phrased. Were the Easter events purely natural or were they "supernatural"? Could not they have been both in ways we do not understand either because they are beyond our understanding or, more likely, because we have yet to grow in sufficient wisdom to understand how that is possible? From the beginning could You not have designed the process so that just once it would produce someone like Jesus who would survive death?

Once we admit the marvelous, the question is, Why not that kind of marvel too?

Anyway this is a day for rejoicing no matter how bad the weather or how gloomy some of the prospects are because Your love is stronger than death and that is what it and indeed everything is all about.

April 16, 1993 — Chicago

My Love,

Yesterday was grim. Bad night's sleep, hard day teaching, then two dear people on the phone with tragic problems, back to back. I did my best, but it seemed to me that I was too physically worn out to absorb their problems the way I ought to have. I feel stretched out. I need someone (You) to talk to.

The last three nights I have been unable to sleep through. So I get up at four, eat breakfast, read the papers, and then go back to bed for another hour or two. It's not the best way to sleep. Moreover, I'm not swimming every day either. I was just too weary to do that yesterday when I came home and the phones stopped ringing.

I must keep trying. I love You.

April 18, 1993 — Chicago

My Love,

Last night when I got back from the seminary about ten o'clock, dead tired, I had hardly sat down when the phone rang, with a priest who wanted to talk, needed to talk. So we talked and I was cordial and friendly, which is what I want to be. But, dear God, I was so exhausted.

Right now I feel that I don't even begin to exist spiritually. Yet I do love You. Help me, please. Do I hear You say that I must help myself? Indeed I must.

April 19, 1993 — Chicago

My Love,

My Easter lilies are beginning to wither. So sad. I feel like the lilies this morning. I didn't sleep much again last night. I'm supposed to go to the Cubs game tonight, but it looks like it will be rained out. I desperately need some rest and peace.

In her talks at the seminary Carol Zaleski talked about sleeping and waking as part of the human condition and as part of the heavenly city — the peace of sleep and the alertness of waking combined. It sounds very attractive because I have neither peace nor alertness at this point. Yet someone who really trusted in Your love would live in this world with a blend of the two that would anticipate a little bit, as a kind of promise or even a down payment, the heavenly rest and the heavenly alertness. If I really believed in Your love and Your affection for me, Your protecting arms around me, I would not be so upset and so tensed out by the combination of projects and worries that are assaulting me.

And I wouldn't feel this Monday morning like a withering Easter lily. You don't want me to be this way and I ought not to be this way.

I'll keep trying. What more can I say?

When Mike Hout was here last night — and it was great to see him and talk to him again — I was way out on overload. I think he might have noticed it. I should not do that to my friends. What am I racing against? I wonder. Maybe I can slow down a bit the next two days after I get the material ready for class on Thursday.

I will not wither like the Easter lily till it is my time to do so, and it's not yet my time.

April 22, 1993 — Chicago

My Love,

I finally got to sleep last night and a good sleep it was, for which I am very grateful. Dear God, what a shambles

I've become, worrying about each night's sleep. It's my own fault for working after supper, something I'll try not to do again.

I have bounced back with little effort from the limited success of the new book. I still can't quite figure it out. There was another huge batch of mail yesterday, all of it favorable. Why does such reaction not translate into sales? As You know it's not me that I worry about but those who have come to depend on me in one way or another. I never intended to get caught this way.

Dry, drained, and dumb — that's how I feel this morning. But I know that despite all that You still love me.

As I try to love You.

April 24, 1993 — Chicago

My Love,

This review [of *Love Affair*] I mentioned the other day was in *Emmanuel*, a magazine for priests, and was most favorable, praising me for honesty, sensitivity, and faith. Now You know and I know that the praise is undeserved. Clerical culture faults me for the novels I haven't written (because they haven't read the ones I have written) and then praises me for virtue that I don't have.

How could anyone read the last three weeks of this journal and not think I was a jerk — except possibly You and love is blind anyway, right? They would say, as did one letter writer, that I have no grounds for complaint because I got myself into the work schedule that put me on extended overload. And they would say that with excellent reason. Even You might think it, but love knows when to be silent, especially since the beloved knows what the lover would say.

Anyway, You and I know the truth about me, and we

also know that I'm not trying to kid anyone in these reflections.

I promise that whatever else I do here, I will return to poems about my friend Moon — Grinning Moon and Easter Moon I will call them. Time that I bring her (Moon, that is) in from the thresholds!

April 25, 1993 — Grand Beach, Michigan

My Love,

It is wonderful to be back here. What an important role this place has played in my life, sometimes sad, even tragic, other times joyous and refreshing. I admit that I have not made good use of it for the latter purposes, though in its absence I might not be alive. Even walking in the house creates a sense of relaxation that I never experience in Chicago.

It's typical late April in the Middle West, maybe a month behind Eliot's "cruelest month" of the year. The grass is green and so are a few of the bushes; an occasional tree springs buds, but most of them are still winter stark. I had to leave U.S. 20 on the way up because a road was closed and drove on U.S. 12 through an unspoiled dune forest. The trees were as stark as they were in November. I'll take that route the next couple of times to watch spring explode — as it does here. Spring can be a week or even a few days, then it's summer — life impatient to be reborn under the fierce warmth of the sun.

The lake is much higher, my stairs washed away. I'll have to search for them. Someone said they saw them down by the sea wall.

I'm quite exhausted. Only when I get here do I realize how beat I am. Help me, I beg You, to use these couple of days here for refreshment and renewal. I love You.

April 26, 1993 — Grand Beach, Michigan

My Love,

Last night I watched the film that June gave me and insisted that I watch — *A Midnight Clear,* the story of six soldiers in the Ardennes at Christmastime in 1944. More than a film about the folly of war, it is about loyalty and love within the squad, and even tenderness among men. It is important — indeed all-important — that men cherish as well as respect women. But it is also important that men cherish other men. Maybe we will get it right with other men only when we first have got it right with women; maybe we won't fight men when we have learned that we don't have to fight women. Maybe when we have learned to be brave enough not to oppress women we can then trust ourselves to be tender — in a different and analogous way. We have a long way to go, but that would make a wonderful theme for a novel, would it not?

April 26, 1993 — Grand Beach, Michigan

My Love,

It only takes a day down here for the pressures to lift and for me to begin to notice You lurking on the margins of life, loving me and loving all those young people in the films.

I love You and am grateful for this wonderful interlude.

May 1993

May 4, 1993 — Grand Beach, Michigan

My Love,

Yesterday I read a line in a book about the universe that is quite striking: "At the heart of the universe is an outrageous bias for the novel, for the unfurling of surprise in prodigious dimensions throughout the vast range of existence."

I used to think of the Big Bang as a huge explosion from which everything else followed inevitably. While that's true, such a model does not reveal the design and the surprise within the design that is structured into the violence and the harmony of the explosion.

Weird, as the kids would say.

The notion that all this is mere accident is simply *not acceptable.* Neither the cosmos nor the tulips blooming outside my window can possibly be accidents. Both however raise the question of what kind of Person could be responsible for the violence and the harmony and the loveliness of the flower.

And for me this raises the question of how I dare address You who ignited the Big Bang with all its order and its wonder as familiarly as I do. How could someone like You care about me? How can I picture You as **vulnerable**?

The answers to those questions are all the same: You reveal Yourself to us as a vulnerable Lover and beg to be loved as such. I dare to address You familiarly because that's the way You want to be addressed.

Why?

No answer to that, is there? Maybe the question is not so much why there is anything at all as why there is love.

I guess with that ultimate mystery we must take the posture of silent and wondering acceptance.

I love You. Help me to love You better.

May 9, 1993, Mother's Day — Chicago

My Love,

We've had our day or two of spring here in Chicago and now it's suddenly summer. When life bursts forth here it does so with incredible vigor. Just a couple of weeks ago when I drove up to St. Mary of the Woods for Mass the trees in the neighborhood and the Forest Preserve were black and bare. Now they are in full bloom, drenched in greenery, and daffodils and tulips are everywhere. The city is unspeakably beautiful and alive with activity and people.

Life, life, life! How powerful it is, how resurgent, how indefatigable, how resourceful, how ingenious, how inventive, how fertile!

It is fitting that we celebrate Mother's Day this time of the year (and hence honor You as our Mother as well as Father). For mothers grant life, just as You do, and their fertility, actual or potential, reveals Your fertility. They are metaphors for life in a way the rest of us cannot be. Yesterday I preached at the parish about violence against women, insisting on respect for the bearers of life as well as for life itself. We Catholics do the latter pretty well and the former badly. The people reacted positively. No one was shocked, no one protested. They know the problem better than we do!

I wish to honor today my own mother, gone these thirty years and more, and not thought of too often consciously, but still of course lurking in my preconscious and unconscious. Not only did I learn about You from her, both in word and more in action, but I also learned about what it means to be a man. What a hard life she had! I hope and believe that You have rewarded her for her goodness and generosity as I could never hope to do.

Much of the attractiveness of women to us men comes from the mystery that they embody, the inviting, appealing mystery that You in Your own maternal ingenuity have made them in order to guarantee the race.

There were two of them in the pool this morning while I was reflecting on these things, not especially young and not especially pretty, but yet, how should I say it, delightful in their womanliness and, I presume, their motherhood. I reflected again on Your ingenuity in designing them and gave thanks for it and for the mystery of life.

You didn't have to make them as lovely as You did and with a loveliness that need not fade with age. But I am grateful that You did.

For that and for all Your other maternal gifts, life-giving blessings, I thank You on this Mother's Day, and I love You.

I also thank You for the good night's sleep.

May 10, 1993 — Chicago

My Love,

I walked back from the birthday/Mother's Day party at Sean and Molly's yesterday, dodging danger from blade runners, skateboarders, bikers, and little kids in strollers — a wonderful melange of early summer. The party was enough to revitalize anyone's savor for life.

It was between three and four, just the time on a hot afternoon that kids become irritable because they haven't had their naps. So, the twins excepted, the kids were generally in no mood to be pleasant. If the sheer physical fertility of women is mysterious and sacramental, how much more impressive is the patient affection that goes into their constant care of their children. Astonishing. Kids can be brats. No, they are brats some of the time because that is the way they are. Mothers still love them. So it must be with You. We are brats and with a lot less justification than little kids. Yet You still love us with patient affection. How generous of You when, as I suppose, You have much better things to do with Your time.

And the flowers are so beautiful this spring-becoming-summer.

I am astonished by You, and I love You.

May 11, 1993 — Chicago

My Love,

The May Crowning at St. Mary of the Woods was truly wonderful. So many memories. Why did we let it almost disappear? Why did we forget her role in our heritage? Why did we forget that she is a metaphor for Your motherly love — so much so that You and she are almost indistinguishable in my imagination because she prepared me to think of You as a mother, in the most important religious experience of my life. One that I didn't even recognize for what it was until just a few days ago I began to write about such experiences in my sociology book.

Thank You for the Mother of Jesus and for her astonishing role in our heritage.

I love You both — and all the other life-giving women in my life.

May 14, 1993 — Chicago

My Love,

The city looks lush these days. As I glance west out of my windows the trees and the lawns are deep green as a result of the combination of rain and sudden heat. Also last night, the air was particularly clear and the city stretching out to the west glistened with clarity and twinkling lights. More beauty for which to thank You.

Wonder lurks everywhere. I may not take much time to notice it, which, as I have said before, is disgraceful. But I am not completely oblivious to it either. Maybe I'm on the verge of being more sensitive to Your grandeur and beauty. I sure hope so.

May 22, 1993 — Chicago

My Love,

I read a poem by Kathleen Norris this morning (Yes, I am getting back to my spiritual reading at long last!) in which she wondered about and prayed for her ancestors and asserted that she felt sure she would see her mother again. Is not this hunger to see again those we loved or those we heard about or those to whom we owe our life a critical part of our motivation to believe in life after death? Does it not finally come down to the issue of whether the creative force responsible for the cosmos could be so cruel as to create beings like us with a hunger to sustain relationships in a life beyond death and deny this hunger?

It might be said that we have no right to yearn for individual immortality, indeed it has been said by some of the best theological minds of our time. However noble and stoic that sentiment may be, it does not work with ordinary people — and I suspect not with the theologians. Norris says that on her deathbed she will expect to see her mother again.

It is the personal and intimate relationship we want to continue, want it so badly that no less a person than William James thought it intolerable that we would not be able to meet our relatives again.

"Intolerable" is the right word, isn't it? "Unacceptable" might be another word. Our hunger to survive has to correspond to a reality, or whoever put that hunger in us is monstrously cruel.

"All manner of things will be well," said Blessed Juliana. I believe her and I believe in You. Ms. Norris's hunger to see her mother again is a hint, a sign, a rumor, a flapping of angels' wings.

I believe that rumor, I take heart from that flap, and I love You.

May 23, 1993 — Chicago

My Love,

This morning I read some poems in the collection of women's poems about death. The first several were about aborted babies and guilt — or perhaps I should say a sense of loss — afterward. I don't know whether the poems reflect the way every such mother feels or even a majority, but that is irrelevant to the fact that some women feel this way. And how could it be otherwise?

I don't like abortion, as You know. I'm not sure however, as You also know, that the Church serves its own goals best by trying to pressure lawmakers.

But again that's not the point either. The point is that the women who wrote those lines lament for lost children, deeply and painfully. I guess I would have known that if anyone asked, but I certainly did not avert to the horror until I read these poems, one by a woman who has had many abortions (and a very well known poet at that). Poor woman. Poor women who have so much harder a time in life than men do.

I'm sure You love these two women. I don't know what comfort there is for them. You will, I know, take care of them.

And my crusade in defense of women will continue, You being willing.

I love You.

May 24, 1993 — Grand Beach, Michigan

My Love,

My reading of poems by women this morning continues to be a chilling experience. How much more they suffer with and for their children. Not merely bringing them into the world, but taking care of them and then working out the strains in the relationships when they become adults.

Men are simply not hard-wired to be that sensitive to parenting. They can learn, however, as I learn from the poems.

And also learn about You. For if You are a bearer of life, You must love us as totally, as hopelessly as the women who wrote these poems. You must suffer terribly when one of Your children suffers, You must grieve when one of them grieves, and You must fight fiercely and passionately to protect them.

If these words are necessarily metaphorical, they fail by defect rather than excess. There are some theological problems involved in these assertions but one must not let theology destroy the metaphor. The big question is why You permit some of Your children to suffer — such as the young Japanese exchange student who was killed by a redneck with a .44 Magnum (the killer being acquitted yesterday).

The only answer, and it has its problems, is that reason which we can't understand: You cannot in the short run stop this suffering.

That's baffling but we must accept it in preference to the alternatives, must we not?

But now I understand even more about the vulnerability of God.

So I must strive to love You more.

May 25, 1993 — Grand Beach, Michigan

My Love,

I returned to reading *The Universe Story* yesterday. The authors say that we have classified two million species of life and that there are between ten and thirty million out there. Moreover billions of other species have gone out of existence, many of them in the four great extinction catastrophes in the earth's history (and some in the various ice ages that have been caused by tilting of the earth's plates). Only 1 percent of the species that ever existed now survive.

There are, they say, eight hundred thousand species of insects, five hundred thousand species of worms, and forty-five hundred species of mammals. They don't add that there is — as far as we know — *only one species of humankind.*

Like, Wow!

So many questions: Why the incredible exuberance of life? Why the violence of the extinctions? Indeed why the violence of the whole business of cosmogenesis? Why the evolutionary process of mutation, natural selection, and niche selection?

And dare we think it is all ordered, all the billions of species, toward one species? If it is, is this not an incredibly elaborate way of doing things, of producing a self-conscious and reflective being that can begin to return Your love?

I can understand the exuberance of the cosmos and of life. My mind boggles at the violence — and at the tiny but apparently critical role that humankind plays in the whole process, though we will be lucky to survive the next ice age, to say nothing of the next extinction.

Are there others like us? The science fiction stories I was reading yesterday assume that there must be. Logically there should be. But You are the kind of creator, with a sense of humor of Your own, who might just like the idea of beings in Your own image and likeness on just one planet and at just one short time in that planet's history.

Where were You — You might ask as the author has You asking poor Job — when I made all this stuff? And who are You to criticize my style?

Not me, Lady Wisdom!

I can wonder, can't I?

But You are surely an exuberant and violent Person.

And a loving one too. Even the birds of the air and the flowers of the field testify to this.

I love You, as I always do. But I fear You too. You're a wild one.

May 27, 1993 — Grand Beach, Michigan

My Love,

Are *we* what it's all about? Somehow it seems arrogant to think that the Big Bang and the violence and exuberance of cosmogenesis were designed just to produce us. However, in fact it *was* designed to produce us. We were locked in from the beginning, which is fascinating. Whether we will be an errant sport of the evolutionary process or not remains to be seen. Whether there will be more evolution (into angel-like creatures as I suggested in one of my novels) also remains to be seen.

But the reflection that occurs to me tonight is that You went to a lot of work, perhaps enjoyable work, certainly exuberant work, and astonishingly violent work to produce us and indeed to produce me. What do You expect of us? What do You expect of me?

I guess the answer to that is love, my Love. Maybe not the greatest response to love that the cosmos has seen (though the greatest capability about that we know), but certainly a being, a person, which has some minor capacity to respond to Your love.

Big task. We can but try.

Help me to love You more.

May 28, 1993 — Grand Beach, Michigan

My Love,

As I reflect on the extraordinary story of this universe that You have given us I become even more astonished at how different You are from the bland, abstract, theoretical God who has been served up by theologians, philosophers, and religious educators — and how much You, as revealed in the cosmos, are like the God of the Scriptures.

You are passion of incredible power and violence and intelligence of astonishing ingenuity. A dangerous lover, a determined lover, a clever lover. There is, however, in the story of the universe nothing about Your vulnerability, which the Scriptures do reveal. How can someone with so much power and so much intelligence also be vulnerable? It seems quite impossible, except that all lovers are vulnerable and that seems to be of the essence of love. Just now, filled with *The Universe Story*, I find myself more than a little afraid of You because of Your power and intelligence. You're dangerous. I'm no match for You, not at all.

But then who is a match for a lover?

Help me to realize that for Your awesome power You are both tender and need tenderness. And thus to love You more and more — and permit You to love me.

May 31, 1993 — Grand Beach, Michigan

My Love,

Last night, after I had finished most of my work on the sociology book, I watched a 1946 film called *The Killers* on A & E. It was rated four stars in the listings, but it wasn't all that good. Techniques have improved enormously since then. The stars were a young Burt Lancaster and a young Ava Gardner. Will they be showing these films a thousand years from now, historical relics that give a vivid insight not to the times but to what kind of entertainment values people had in 1946?

And will they still think a thousand years from now that Ava Gardner (You be good to her) was beautiful? Standards of beauty are said to change with the times.

The poor woman is dead now, a tragic person despite her beauty and her fame, lonely and seemingly unloved at the end. All her beauty is dust, the lot of all human beauty and intelligence and insight and talent. All in the grave-yard with the young men who died in the folly of war and whom we remember today.

And, if the ecological activists are to be believed, we are not likely to survive a thousand years anyway.

Grim thoughts this early morning as the wind howls in off the lake and ten-foot waves assault the shoreline. But Memorial Day is a time for grim thoughts, thoughts of blighted youth and lost loves and early death and later death, but especially of death.

It is also a time to think of resurrection if I believe in You, of all of us as young and laughing again, of 1946 and our being eighteen. I do believe in You, and I do believe that death does not have the last word. Life is too impor-tant ever to be anything but life, despite all the seeming evidence to the contrary.

I *do* love You.

June 1993

June 2, 1993 — Grand Beach, Michigan

My Love,

Forgiveness heals all our wounds, Alice Walker says in the poem I read this morning. The poems in this section are all about death and dying, which is something that will happen to me sooner rather than later. I do not want to die without all the forgiveness sought and given. There are some things that must be cleared up, though in truth I don't know how to go about it. I have tried and failed in some relationships and not tried in others. One must wait the appropriate time. One must also respect those who don't want relationships renewed, as I have tried to do.

About some of these things I don't know. One I must take care of at Christmas this year, because that's the time to do it, especially if I follow my resolution of going on a retreat the week before Christmas.

I don't know how to do some of these things, but I know they must be done. Help me to do them.

I love You.

June 4, 1993 — Grand Beach, Michigan

My Love,

The poems I've been reading from the book are all in a section called "Generations" but really should be called "Death." They are brilliant, sensitive, poignant poems. Women are not only better novelists then men, they are also better poets. They note all the details and turn many of them into metaphors that a man would never see — the way a woman scans a kitchen and sees mess that a man doesn't see or, rather, just barely sees but does not really notice.

I don't know whether this ability to see is cultural or genetic and I don't much care. It is powerful and important and a rich resource.

So the poems on death are as poignant and sad as any I have ever read. Moreover, in some cases they are also filled with faith, not all but some. It's a faith I need as I grow older.

I love You. Help me to love You more.

June 9, 1993 — Grand Beach, Michigan

My Love,

The book of poems turns from death to alienation, "brokenness" as the editor calls it. Not cheery stuff, to put it mildly. But very good poetry. As usual women are so much better than men at sensing the tiny and significant details of a situation — and the personal horror. It makes me wonder this morning whether You're one of them, in league with them, conspiring with them against us. I'm joking, of course, but You are the one who is responsible for the details of creation and presumably You are sensitive to those details, just like women are. They are better novelists and better poets because of that sensitivity which, to be serious rather than flippant, reflects Your sensitivity, Your agony over individual horror, Your feel for personal suffering. Another argument for Your maternal and womanly vulnerability.

One of the poems this morning is by Your friend Hildegard of Bingen, whose marvelous music I'm enjoying. What a woman she must have been! Still is, for that matter. She could have run the whole world in those days, better than the men who were trying to run it. In the poem she laments that so many people who were supposed to "grow green" have withered and turned brown. A woman's cry, a mother's cry, a lament for the lost children who might have been something, but are almost nothing because their promise has been swept away by the troubles and agonies, by the brokenness of life.

Why do You permit that breaking-up to happen? "It isn't fair," a woman cries out in another poem this morning. Why indeed? That I don't know, but I do know that You suffer with every single broken human being. As I said at the start of one of my novels, "It's hell to be God." You suffer so much with Your children. I wish I could stop some of the breaking. I've tried, as You know, and failed. If I feel anguish about those failures, how much anguish must You feel.

I love You.

June 11, 1993 — Grand Beach, Michigan

My Love,

The reading from Isaiah this morning reminds me of the crisis in the Church over pedophilia. There are tens of thousands of survivors of clerical abuse out there, and increasingly they have the courage to come forward. And the safe, conservative men the Vatican has sent to the American Church are too dumb to know what to do. So they'll drift aimlessly, issuing self-serving statements and following the instructions of inept legal advisers.

I bet that really infuriates You, especially since they're doing it all in Your name!

I will not turn away from my involvement with the problem, because I believe You would never forgive me if I did (well, You forgive everything, but You know what I mean). But I find it all very depressing, as I'm sure You do too.

Anyway, I love You very much (the words of love stick in the throat, as a couple of women poets remark this morning). Help the Church escape the folly of its leaders.

June 12, 1993 — Grand Beach, Michigan

My Love,

The poems this morning and the reading in Isaiah converge. The poems are about women who have been abused, and the reading from the prophet is about purification of the dross of infidelity and corruption from Jerusalem. In my world just now the corruption of abuse, and especially the abuse of children by priests, is a terrible dross that must be purified from the Church. I continue to be dismayed by the infidelity of the hierarchy and of so many of my fellow priests, their pretense that the problem does not exist, their insensitivity to the suffering of the victims, their pathetic ignorance of the anger of the lay people. Fools! Blind, stupid fools! Fomenters of anti-Catholicism! Harlots!

I feel so frustrated because I am now aware that no matter what happens, the folly will continue. No matter how many revelations there are, no matter how much stench rises from the body ecclesiastic, nothing will happen, nothing will change. Their office and position and power and clout with the Vatican will remain secure if they do absolutely nothing, and they will do absolutely nothing, nothing at any rate that is responsive to the problem. They will mouth some pieties, say some utterly foolish things, issue a bland statement and set up a committee. That's all!

Well, I'm not the sword of Yourself. I can only continue to say what I believe is true and leave the rest to You. But I hate to see the work of American Catholicism, with so much good in it despite its flaws, be brought down because of the idiots who are our leaders.

I do love You. Protect us all from evil.

I love You.

June 21, 1993 — Grand Beach, Michigan

My Love,

The Bulls won last night in the last three seconds of the game! So, as usual when I'm stimulated after supper, I fall asleep and wake up about now. I'm glad the playoffs are over. I can relax. Beatrice Bruteau insists in her book [*Radical Optimism*] that we must practice stillness and silence, as did the monastic contemplatives. The point is well taken. I will be aware of You and of my own real self to the extent that I am able to be still and silent, at peace, at ease, at rest. She argues that one must avoid too much stimulation — drink, tobacco, rich food, even caffeine. Maybe I drink too much tea and too much Coke. No, I *surely* do, in part when I'm fasting. One pot of tea a day should be enough. I can always drink water or raspberry soda, which doesn't have caffeine.

Ironic that I should be reflecting on these things when

I'm awake in the small hours because of excessive stimulation from a basketball game!

I was silent and still for a time on the beach today, listening to the waves and the wind and feeling the breeze and the warmth. I was aware of Your presence, however briefly and with however many distractions.

I am dismayed that I have not done that for a long time.

On these nights when I am overstimulated for one reason or another I probably should take a walk to relax instead of collapsing into bed.

Most of this is mechanical, but as a beginner I must concentrate on the mechanical.

Bruteau also says that in addition to talking to You I should shut up and listen, not necessarily to what You *say* but just listen to *You*. Let God be silent, she says. That's a good idea, but I think I also should give You a chance to talk.

Help me to do these things in the days ahead.

I love You.

June 23, 1993 — Grand Beach, Michigan

My Love,

Why T-Rex?

That's my question after seeing *Jurassic Park*.

Indeed why the dinosaurs at all? Why the raptors? Why 160 million years of such weirdos? The experiment was unsuccessful, as You knew it was going to be, so why try it? And then why let it go on so long?

I personally think those are good questions — not that I expect answers.

If one is to judge You by Your deeds, and that seems legitimate enough, why those deeds? You're an odd one, that's for sure.

The response might well be that the process has a logic of its own and that You work out Your designs through the process. T-Rex was part of the process. But what did they tell us about You?

Still no answers. I know the Job response: I wasn't around while You were making the universe, so I should mind my own business. I admit that. Still I want to see how this long process of evolutionary creation reveals something about You — other than Your ability to achieve Your goals in and through the process.

Which is maybe enough.

Are we a goal? Some evolutionary biologists argue that we are just part of the ongoing process and that we will eventually go the way of the dinosaurs, either at the time of the next great extinction or before that through our own folly — and in a lot less time than sixty million years. The process, they say, has no goal other than its own continuation.

Except that we are qualitatively different because we can know reflectively and love.

I wish the theologians whose job it is to explain such things would try to dialogue with the scientists in some sort of creative fashion about these things. But they're too involved in what they think is politics.

It was very clever of Spielberg's technical goons to produce those artificial dinosaurs. How much more clever to produce the real thing. Was it all a show for us? Or for whoever comes after us?

Maybe?

I'm baffled. And I'm also in awe.

And I love You.

June 24, 1993 — Grand Beach, Michigan

My Love,

I continue to ponder the dinosaurs — 160 million years of those strange creatures! The question that occurs to me this morning is not how someone with that kind of time perspective and that apparent fascination with huge beings (T-Rex could do forty miles an hour!) could be concerned with me.

I can begin to grasp that: any God who can't be concerned about every one of his creatures (the very hairs of your head are numbered!) would not be much of a God, would She?

Love can't be explained, I guess. I suppose You were fond of T-Rex for all his strange ways. A nice pet, maybe. Or at least a revelation of Your power. (What do You think of Barney, I wonder? Most parents don't like him, but I bet You do.) We're not nearly so much to look at — or maybe we are, I don't know. But we are more than pets. We're lovers, almost whether we want to be or not. Go figure, as they say.

I thought of You the other night when I watched Fellini's *La Notte* on satellite. Jeanne Moreau, whom I had never seen before in a film, was a powerful image of smouldering vulnerability. My age, she was thirty-two when the film was made, around long enough to know what a broken heart is and also long enough to be a bundle of hungers. Is that what You're like?

A dangerous metaphor perhaps, but a valid one, I think.

I love You.

June 27, 1993 — Grand Beach, Michigan

My Love,

Dreams last night about impossible tasks, working with a computer macro, trying to find a place in an unfamiliar suburb without directions or a good map, and trying to make a TV assignment when I didn't know where to go and was in a traffic jam.

Probably all the result of trying to arrange for a dinner party and do Mass on the dune at the same time — an impossible challenge made worse by the rain that hovered around all day. (I mean, seriously, isn't it time for the rain to stop!) But I suspect the dreams, which I know I've had before in some form, also reveal a basic personality structure, a conviction that I am obligated to do the almost impossible. One mixes that with the fear of enemies lurking with knives and one gets a pretty driven person, and a person with lots of latent anger.

It is not a portrait I'm prepared to question. I know You love me just the same and I know that dreams exaggerate and overstate. But they are very useful for self-knowledge. These underlying personality structures can't be changed, but they can be modified and redirected, which is one of the things my spiritual life ought to be about.

Now back to my guests.

I love You.

June 29, 1993 — Grand Beach, Michigan

My Love,

Last night's dream had be involved in a sinister mystery in a resort hotel. Threatened by danger with an obligation to protect other people. Maybe the result of the film *Lifepod*, a takeoff on the old *Lifeboat* from ages ago.

But again revelatory of who and what I am. It's astonishing how much one can learn, or perhaps relearn, in a few nights' dreams. How much of my involvement in causes in the Church comes from this sense of responsibility that is so deeply built into my soul. I wanted to save Chicago from [Cardinal] Cody. Then I wanted to save the Church from the pedophilia mess. Who am I to mess with such problems? Why do I see myself as the only one who cares about them?

June 29, 1993 — Grand Beach, Michigan

My Love,

My father's son? Surely he would be proud of my involvement in both, just as he was involved in so many similar projects.

I'm not saying that this idealism or compulsion or whatever it might be called is all bad. It's the way You made me. Don Quixote, as the young people from Christ the King used to call me. Surely the pedophile fight is Quixotish. Yet *some* priest should take the stand I have. I would do it all again, though, if I could, with less emotional involvement. The point here is that it would have been very helpful if I was aware of the drive to responsibility, and perhaps to omnipotence, had been clear in my head as a wild energy that was at work.

You may not like this reflection. You could say that I'm being too hard on myself, perhaps trying to impress You. I don't think so. I'm not saying my propensity to crusade is bad. I'm saying rather that it is an impulse that must be treasured and followed wisely. I don't regret the criticism of Cody. Nor do I regret my stand on pedophilia. I take little satisfaction from people now saying I've been right all along. I'd rather have been right *without* the publicity. I must, however, beware of being carried away by my own enthusiasms.

Anger, enthusiasm, striving for the impossible — those are currents within myself that I recognize again after only three nights of dreams. A profitable analysis in self-understanding. Potential blessings, potential curses, depending on how I respond to them.

I love You. Help me to respond wisely.

July 1993

July 1, 1993 — Grand Beach, Michigan

My Love,

Poor Anne Sexton, in a lovely poem I read yesterday, describes the wonder and the surprise, the presence of Yourself in the things she wakes up to in the morning. Maybe she was more of a morning person than I am. It takes me a while to be aware of even myself, much less of anyone else as I bounce (however reluctantly) out of bed. If I don't bounce, I don't get up, as You well know.

But let me try. I find You in the taste of the cereal, especially if there is fruit on it, in the crunch of the flakes, in the sweetness of the raisins, in the reassurance of my first morning cup of tea, in the sound of the birds (pretty quiet these days), in the warmth of the sunlight, in the moments of peace while I read the paper and listen to WFMT, in the hope of a new day, in the ideas I have from last night, in the wisdom of my spiritual reading, and in these often hasty and ill-expressed reflections.

If one can see sacraments in the morning, then one can see them any time.

I can look out the window and see the green of the lawn (almost like Ireland it is so green) and dull brilliance of the flourishing flowers, and I know You are still around.

It would be generous of You to get rid of that front that has laid over us like a pall for two weeks and still threatens us for many more weeks. Stop the rain, not only for my Fourth but for the poor farmers. Please!

Note how I justify my insistence with concern for others!

Anyway help be to be aware of Your presence in the events of this day and this long weekend.

I love You.

July 4, 1993 — Grand Beach, Michigan

My Love,

Thank You for the blessings of American freedom, peace, and prosperity.

I love You.

July 8, 1993 — Grand Beach, Michigan

My Love,

Bill Quinn and Bob Barron were here yesterday and today, and as usual with both of them I learn a lot.

Bob is very strong in his convictions about the central role of the priesthood in the Church. Would that every priest was as enthusiastic as he is and with an enthusiasm as well grounded in sound theology. It gives me a boost in my morale just to spend some time with a priest who thinks about the priesthood the way I do but with the energy of youth and despite all the disillusioning experiences of our era.

He is right: this is a *kairos* moment, a time of crisis and a time of opportunity, if only enough priests could see that as to break out of the bonds of clerical culture.

I must not give up hope.
I love You. Strengthen my hope.

July 9, 1993 — Grand Beach, Michigan

My Love,
How good of You to produce raspberries. They are a wondrous sacrament, a surprise every time the first ones of the season appear.
I love You.

July 14, 1993 — Grand Beach, Michigan

My Love,
Last night I had supper with some of my friends of my generation. They remarked that I seemed not terribly discouraged by all the mess in the Church. I guess I'm not. Concerned, yes. Angry, yes. But I don't think the Church is in terminal trouble, not as long as we have good laity (like my friends) out in the parishes. That's where the hope is. That indeed is where You are.
I love You.

July 26, 1993 — Grand Beach, Michigan

My Love,
You planted a wonderful idea in my head yesterday for the next book, indeed for the next four books — a cycle to be called *A Catholic Quartet*. Grant that it will work, please.
I love You. Thanks again for the idea and for the nice day.

July 31, 1993 — Grand Beach, Michigan

My Love,

I had a letter yesterday from a woman who was at her wit's end. Terrible guilt, temptation to suicide, awful image of You as the Great Punisher. You're not that way. What terrible distortions of You we have presented to our people. Help her, I beg You.

And a poignant thing on TV last night. A woman received a half century late the final letter from her husband, written before he was killed in the war. She had never remarried. No children. What suffering. Yet You love her and all the others whom I worry about today. You love me too. More than any human love. I must trust in that love.

I love You. Help me to love You more.

August 1993

August 3, 1993 — Grand Beach, Michigan

My Love,

In one of the poems I read this morning, You are depicted as being fed up with us and responding to our demands that You show us a sign with a demand that we show You. I don't think You're that kind of person, any more than You are the vengeful God of the fundamentalists (punishing riverboat gambling with the Mississippi flood, according to their most recent pronouncements!). Yet there must be many times when You feel something not unlike our discouragement.

You also understand how fragile we are and frightened, how tenuous our existence and uncertain our future, how problematic our lives and how ephemeral our loves. We are afraid, my Love, terrified. So You must forgive us much of what we do because, as Your son said, we don't really know what we are doing.

Not that we are completely innocent either. But we are still children, naughty, nervous, unhappy little children.

However, we are *Your* children. You love us. We may be all You have. Even if we're not, we're still Yours. Take care of us and continue to love us. And love me, frightened little boy child that I am. I love You.

August 4, 1993 — Grand Beach, Michigan

My Love,

I guess I didn't expect the papal visit to Denver to stir up so much media attention. But I forgot it was August when nothing happens in the news, except an occasional war or revolution. I was bugged all day yesterday by calls from media folks, most of whom are bent on replaying the paradigms of a quarter century ago. They don't seem to realize that the laity and the lower clergy resolved the birth control issue long ago and that, while Catholics like the Pope, they do not listen to him when sex is the issue. I fear my patience is wearing thin with such ignorance.

Will they ever learn that Catholics stay Catholic because they like being Catholic!

Anyway, I love You. Take care of the Pope on his trip.

August 8, 1993 — Grand Beach, Michigan

My Love,

In one of the poems this morning You are compared to an endless field of wheat, not an original metaphor but nonetheless a powerful one. I could just as well compare You to Lake Michigan, that deep, huge, unpredictable, awesome, lovely, astonishing lake.

Which will not calm down enough this summer for me to waterski on it. But that's another matter.

However, on this lazy Sunday morning, I am not very happy with myself. There is a tangle of confusion in my mind, problems, worries, fears, uncertainties that I think are at odds with what I preach and teach and what I believe. It is not merely the dog days of August and there are, as You well know, things worth being concerned about. One of my guests said at supper last night that I looked better than I had in years. Either appearances are deceiving or I must have looked pretty awful.

What discourages me the most, however, is that I make so little of the beauty and joy all around me. That's blind, stupid, and dumb, and I'm sorry.

Today on the beach I will indeed turn to poetry. Maybe that will help me out as it has in the past.

I do love You. Help me to continue to relax and pull me out of my mood — and I hope the two petitions are not incompatible.

August 9, 1993 — Grand Beach, Michigan

My Love,

No poems yesterday. They simply wouldn't come. But I reviewed down on the beach — a beautiful August Sunday — the reasons for my low morale: Jack's sickness, no contract for the novel, rejection of a couple of articles, the ebbing of summer, and the ebbing of my life. What, I asked myself, would cheer me up? A contract in early September? I haven't been worrying explicitly about that, but I suppose all that it implies has been preying on my unconscious, as well as the question of how long I must fight against bigotry and prejudice and lies.

The answer to the last is that it is a fight that will never be won and I shouldn't expect it will be.

But the answer to all the problems is that I have had in the last couple of years enough signs of Your great love that I shouldn't be in this slough of depression. As I said recently, if others can see You in the wheat field, so I should be able to see You in the lake.

I must trust in Your love. But saying that is not enough. My problems are finally not intellectual or doctrinal. They are spiritual and existential. Ultimately they concern the value of my life and my work, which are matters that cannot be judged. If I'm tired, it is not a physical weariness but a spiritual one. I'm not sure how to pull myself out of it. Help me, please.

Thank You for the birth of my fourth grandniece yesterday, a certain Brigit (sic) Clare. May this little creature of light flourish long and happily. May her light shine upon her family.

I love You.

August 13, 1993 — Grand Beach, Michigan

My Love,

A terrible day yesterday. I made the mistake of agreeing to go on *Night Line*, and they harassed me all day long and then managed the hook-up five minutes before the program went off the air. The *Sun Times* wanted a new column — on the Pope, not on the White Sox. Phones all day long. The next time the Pope comes to America (and he surely radiates charm), I hope it's not while I'm on vacation!

But I did get down to the beach and worked on a few haiku:

> Sky and lake turn gray
> Sound of thunder in the distance
> Smell of dead fish

> Skimming the smooth lake
> Two white cruisers race for home
> Before the storm comes

> Pope and president
> Meet under the Rockies' rain
> Talk past each other

Tomorrow off to Denver, after two Masses here, for TV. I don't want to do that either.

Help me. I love You.

August 14, 1993 — Grand Beach, Michigan

My Love,

The Pope has not apologized for the pedophile mess. I didn't think he would. What a terrible mistake.

August 20, 1993 — Grand Beach, Michigan

My Love,

In my research on the spirituality of marriage I discovered that those men and women who think their spouse is like You are those who are especially likely to picture the spouse as "exciting," "romantic," and "mysterious." (And a "sharp dresser." That's an interesting metaphor for You, isn't it, especially since it is an unconscious metaphor?).

Fair enough, though. You are surely mysterious and exciting and romantic too. As for being a sharp dresser, is not creation Your garment? And how could anything be sharper than that?

I have argued for a long time that we had to pay more attention to the religious experience of the laity. Now we have data on that experience that is particularly valuable because it is an experience in what is often taken to be a secular context, marital love. We ought to do a lot with it. The God who is the lover is the God of the Scriptures, if not the God of the theologians.

I love You.

August 23, 1993 — Grand Beach, Michigan

My Love,

On the way to Chicago for a doctor's appointment.
Grant that all goes well. I trust completely in Your love and
care for me and accept whatever You have in Your plans.
Grant that I may learn to live better with ambiguity and
uncertainty.

I love You.

August 25, 1993 — Grand Beach, Michigan

My Love,

> Radiant in sunlight
> A boat in full sail slips by
> Eucharist on the dune
>
> Monarch butterfly
> Lands on the rusty sea wall
> On her journey home
>
> Eager red dog barks
> At placid gold retriever
> Who refuses to play
>
> Tiny twin daughters
> Hand in hand face the rollers
> Screech when bowled over

I hope You like my sacraments.
I love You.

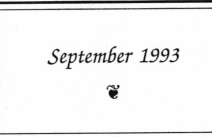

September 1993

September 1, 1993 — Grand Beach, Michigan

My Love,

September already! How quickly the months of summer slipped away. Now I'm going back to work, revising a novel even though there is no contract for it. I ask for Your help and support.

Hans [Küng] typically was in good form the other night, and more mellow than he has been in a long time. But he is very concerned about the next conclave because, quite rightly, he sees the fate of the conciliar reforms very much at issue.

We are, he said, the last men of the Council. That kind of took my breath away. But in truth the bishops and theologians who made the Council are either dead or inactive. I'm hardly a man of the Council in the sense that he is. He was an active figure for all four sessions. I was a tourist at one session.

But my life was shaped by the Council, and my work through the years dedicated to its spirit. Indeed my work was based on the assumption that the Church had really changed.

Perhaps it has, but not nearly enough, as the recent papal visit showed.

Küng wonders whether we will live to see the Council vindicated. He thinks there's a chance. I'm not so sure. Indeed, after two Popes who disappointed us so badly, I am not at all optimistic. I know that it will be vindicated in the end. In the meantime life goes on, and I have a book to revise and contracts to worry about.

Still I pray for him and for the spirit in the Church to which both of us have dedicated our lives, each of us in our own and somewhat different way.

September 3, 1993 — Grand Beach, Michigan

My Love,

I'm discouraged this morning, indecisive about what to do with the day. I've been thinking about how important the summer holidays are in my novel, especially the one I'm revising now, and how dreadful this weekend is surely going to be with family grief, bad weather, conflicting obligations, and general unease about the novels themselves.

I ought not to be worried about the novels. They are no longer the bestsellers they used to be, but people still read then in very large numbers and benefit from them. I still earn enough from them to sustain my commitments to others and not to have to worry about personal money. I still have fun writing them. In fact, I regret not having written one in more than a year. I will turn to writing fiction again when I'm in Tucson and have unloaded the enormous burden of sociology writing, which has occupied me for the last year.

So I should not feel discouraged or disheartened today. But I do. Maybe most of it's the weather.

Or the crazy day that yesterday was — pedophilia (a visitor and a phone call), the archdiocese, sociology of religion, computer problems, fiction revisiting all rushed into a crowded day and a crowded week.

I won't go on. You know how I feel, and You love me just the same. And I love You, and it will get better, and eventually "all will be well and all manner of things will be well."

September 5, 1993 — Grand Beach, Michigan

My Love,

I'm spiritually dry these days, drier than usual that is. Maybe when I settle down next week to a fairly regular routine for the next three weeks and get my spiritual life back in order, things will be better. For the moment I must be content with saying that I love You and I know that You love me and that all will be well. Eventually.

September 9, 1993 — Grand Beach, Michigan

My Love,

The poems I read this morning are about "remything" — retelling biblical tales in modern idiom to bring them alive again, often for ideological purposes. There is one by Job's wife demanding to know where her children are, a reasonable complaint but one that misses the point of the story. I'm not sure the poems are all that successful either as biblical or modern stories. As You know, I've always felt that one must depart from the biblical format to tell stories about You. Or at least that I had to. When Jack Shea does his narrative interpretation of the Bible stories, the result is very powerful indeed. Why should stories of grace be so hard to tell? Because people don't believe in grace any more? But some of the *poets* do believe.

I think the stories should always be about surprise, because that's what You are — the biggest surprise of all. I try to make my stories about the surprises of second chances, which seem to me to be the biggest wonders of all. There are some people who are for one reason or another are incapable of taking the opportunities offered by second chance. But a lot more could than actually do. Why not? Pride and fear, which are the same thing. I must, if I am to be consistent with my own stories, seize all of them that come my way.

Another and very classy publisher is interested in my Catholic Quartet concept. I hope that it works out. Grant that it will. It will keep me pretty busy, but it will also be fun.

I love You. Help me to love You more. Even if summer is fading on us!

September 10, 1993 — Grand Beach, Michigan

My Love,

I just read a quote from *Report to Greco* by Nikos Kazanztakis. God is the cry within us, he says, driving us on, the amphibians to get out of the mud and to transcend ourselves.

You are more than that (though I'm not sure Nikos would have agreed). But You are at least that, a loud violent wind — like the one blowing off the Lake this morning — screaming at everything that has happened since the Big Bang to get up and get moving. It's a cry that I seem to find more difficult and demanding every morning of my life. I would so like to read the papers and then sink into a book, to ignore the phone and the mail, and not to do anything at all.

Of course I will respond to the cry as long as You

give me life and health. The habits of a lifetime do not suddenly stop.

But now I have come to believe that the cry is not an order so much as an invitation, a love song that sings, "Come to me!"

I believe that, my Beloved. Help me to respond to Your cry of love.

September 13, 1993 — Grand Beach, Michigan

My Love,

One does not need comfort when one has purpose; one does not need pleasure when one has meaning — so one of the quotations in the spiritual reading his morning. And another points out that if we are asked what we would most like to have and are granted it, then it will soon not be enough to keep us happy.

In the late 1970s, if someone had predicted *per impossibile* to me that I would be a highly successful novelist, I would have responded that it would have been enough and more than enough to make the rest of my life serene and happy. Of course, it did not do so, nor has anything else nor could anything else. Success, acclaim, impact are not enough, not even if they didn't bring along their inevitable companions, envy and hatred.

So meaning and purpose are really the only things that can keep a person going and reasonably satisfied. I know that to be true, and I have learned it through experience. But there is more to be said, though perhaps it falls under the "meaning and purpose" rubric. The secret of happiness in life, that which finally gives it meaning and purpose, is to feel that someone is seeking You, longing for You, dreaming about You. In this respect more than anything else, human lovers are sacraments for You. It is hard to comprehend and perhaps even harder to integrate within oneself that You are seeking me, longing for me, dreaming about me. Yet I believe it to be true because You Yourself have said that it is true. I do not understand the theology of it and perhaps never will, not even in the world to come. But I do believe that You are longing for me. Help me, my Love, please help me to respond to that longing and find it the meaning and purpose of my life.

September 14, 1993 — Grand Beach, Michigan

My Love,

No one can figure out Your game plan, and it is not clear that we will be able to figure it out even in the world that is to come. So many random events that are alleged to fit somehow in Your plan. I don't get it.

Then You pull off something spectacular, something miraculous like the Arab-Israeli agreement, which was signed yesterday, and one wonders what You'll do next. Grant that it may continue and prosper and work.

I love You. Help me to love You more.

September 16, 1993 — Grand Beach, Michigan

My Love,

I began to listen to Jack Shea's tapes yesterday. They are a much better spiritual resource than the new stack of books I have started to read. He spoke of the treasure buried within, the surprise wine cellar with precious wines, the closet full of unopened gifts, most of which might be handkerchiefs but one is an antique watch. Nice metaphors. There is indeed a hidden treasure within me.

The cry that Kazantzakis spoke about in the passage I read the other day is that treasure screaming. It is the fine point of my person, that place where Your Spirit speaks to my spirit. The secret, magic cellar where I could encounter wondrous treasures and surprises is that place where You seek to interact with me. It is the place where You lurk in the depth of me.

Intermittently I am in touch with You in that magic cellar. But I have not really learned how to sustain that contact with You. I have tried, as You well know. I hope to try more and better this summer, but the summer was swept away, as has been my life by demands and obligations — and the attractiveness of my work.

Yet I must continue to struggle to spend more time with You in the treasure trove within me. Perhaps listening to the tapes and reflecting on them every day will help. It will be hard, however, especially when I return a week from today to the maelstrom of life in Chicago.

But if I really believe that You are waiting for me, calling me, inviting me, even pleading with me to come down to the basement, then maybe You will see me down there a little more. Help to try.

I love You.

September 17, 1993 — Grand Beach, Michigan

My Love,

On the tape I listened to yesterday Jack says that the discovery of the third eye, that vision which sees with the eye of the flesh and the eye of the mind but also sees the transcendent, is something that comes and goes and is not a matter of will. Spirituality is a quest for that eye, so we can see the magic cellar down in the basement. I guess I see with it occasionally, though not very often, because I try too hard. You know how hard I've tried through the years and with what little success. I guess I have tried to make it by an act of will and hard work, like I have done everything else in my life. But what's the alternative to the will? Listening, I suppose. The very thing that I have urged on the Church I don't do myself in relationship with You. There's not much contemplative skill in my personality. But to truly see, to find You and Your spirit where You lurk in my house, I must listen more, and that can't be an act of the will either. Rather it has to be an act of letting go.

How much of that did I do this summer?

Hardly any.

I'm sorry.

But I still love You. Take care of me in Chicago.

September 20, 1993 — Grand Beach, Michigan

My Love,

Something to thank You for that I haven't mentioned before. A week ago I was pulling out of the slanted parking slot at the drug store in New Buffalo. A woman cut in front of me and swerved into a parking place. I stomped on the brakes and stopped about three inches from her little girl in the right front seat. The driver was obviously in a hurry. Another couple of inches and both cars would have been smashed and her child injured. A scary experience for me. A couple of angels (which are stories about Your individual love) were working overtime. For which many, many thanks.

I love You. Help me to go on and to recapture some of my old vigor.

September 23, 1993 — Grand Beach, Michigan

My Love,

One of the major themes in Jack's theology is that each of us is the beloved child and that Your son Jesus knows what we are like because he knows what he is like. Therefore, the Gospels are about us. So in the tapes I heard yesterday he applies this to the temptations of Jesus and argues that as beloved children we can no more than Jesus expect to be always full, always powerful, and always safe. It's a nice way of rearticulating an old idea. There are no guarantees for us, at least no short-run guarantees, even if we are the beloved children. Life will not always be safe or secure or full, but just as Jesus did we can survive till the long-run guarantees cut in.

Same old line, my Love, not that I don't believe it. The long run had better be good. But then I'm not the only one who has told You that, am I?

Someone said to me the other day that I have had a nice life and I have no grounds for complaint. That I've had a nice life is beyond doubt, and I acknowledge that and am grateful. But that fact does not lessen the strain of particular situations or the tensions of particular crises or the attacks from those who resent what they think my life is like.

I am no more immune from those things than Jesus was. I have no cause for complaint, but I do have cause for prayers of petition, which I reserve the right to make. As a lover I assume You want to hear my petitions. So I will keep on making them, asking for the things I need, even if what I need is much less than what others need and, in a certain sense, they have more of a right to ask for it than I do.

Speaking of complaints, it's one more windy, gray, rainy day today. Summer is gone now, officially and in every other way. Tomorrow is my last night here. I go home reluctantly — and resentfully when I look at the calendar and the demands that will intrude on my life for the next six weeks before my trip to Europe. Well, I agreed with them all.

Anyway, I love You. Help me to be more loving.

September 26, 1993 — Chicago

My Love,

I have spent a lot of time the last two days trying to get the computer to work right and have finally given it up as a bad job.

But I did go to the Bears game today and enjoyed their decisive victory.

Off to New York tomorrow to talk to Connie Chung about angels. I'll try to make the point that they represent Your love for us as individuals, the kind of love that in Jack's tape yesterday Your son tried to explain to Nicodemus. He did not come to tell people what the criteria of judgment was; rather he came to explain that there was no judgment, only love. I must understand the depth of that truth which must be seen by the third eye to be fully appreciated. No judgment, only love, love without end, passionate love, overwhelming love. How far that vision is from the terrible condition of the Church these days as we hold our breath waiting for another encyclical while the archdiocese totters on the brink of financial destruction. I just wrote a bitter column blaming the failure on the insensitivity of priests. It's not an exaggeration either. When the people like their priest, that cancels out all the other problems and the contributions go up. But too many priests just don't get it.

However, I'm not supposed to be reflecting on the

problems of others but on my own problems, my own Nicodemus-like failure to get it: to comprehend that it's all about love. Like in the parables of these past weeks. You are love, and that's the whole story. I'll be going to New York with a nervous feeling because of the problems with the book contract. That's not what I should be thinking. I should rather be delighted at all the people who have benefited from my novels, even if their era is coming to an end.

But, in truth, I don't believe they are coming to an end. And I love You.

September 29, 1993 — Chicago

My Love,

There is a big storm, trailing a threatening cloud, headed right at me, indeed right at the monitor on my computer. I know You haven't got it in for me, so I'm continuing to write as the storm closes in. But I can understand why my ancestors were scared by such storms. It's one of those "end-of-the-world" days.

I went off with Jack Shea to see *King of the Hill* today, knowing very well what I was getting into by seeing a film about the Great Depression. It was set in 1933, sixty years ago. Brrr...how easy it is to forget consciously and how hard to forget unconsciously what those terrible years were like. Yet there was neither famine nor plague, so there must have been worse years in human history. I suppose what made it really bad for everyone was that it followed a period of prosperity. The most painful part of the film was the poor father, unable to take care of his sick wife and shamed sons.

Well, we escaped the Depression finally, at least most of us did, though there are still pockets of people in our country for whom the Depression economy persists, and there are still men out of work, losing their masculine identity because they cannot find work, and there are still kids who have to live by deceit and by street crime if they are to survive.

While the problems are intricate, they are still intolerable in our society.

Some of the critiques of the Clinton health plan are that it is "socialized medicine" and another "entitlement." Smear words to describe a national policy decision that everyone has the right to health care, a modest enough decision in an affluent society and one that's long overdue. Still one can understand the workers' fear of NAFTA, the other Clinton policy initiative of the moment, as a threat to their jobs. It almost certainly is not, and those who stir up the fear are irresponsible. I will have to write a column on these subjects and take the stand that the Church would take if it was not afraid of the abortion issue, with which the leadership is obsessed.

None of which is what is really on my mind or what will give me nightmares. I think rather of my parents and what they suffered (not as bad as the family in the film but bad enough). How gallant they were and how important what they passed on to me despite their suffering. I hope You have taken good care of them. No, I know You have and that we will all laugh again.

And for that, among other things, I love You.

P.S. The storm seems to be slipping by!

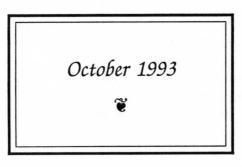

October 1993

October 2, 1993 — Chicago

My Love,

Jack's tape yesterday — the scene in the house of Simon the Pharisee — was about forgiveness, or rather more specifically about forgiving yourself because you perceive yourself as the beloved child. At first I thought that, well, it didn't apply to me all that much because I am not especially guilt-ridden. But the truth is much deeper than that. I don't feel particularly like I am a beloved child. Maybe all the frantic work I do is designed to win a love I don't feel.

I overstate the case. I am much more aware now than I was when I was a newly ordained that I am loved, though it always surprises me to find out how much I seem to mean to other people (and also to discover that with the love I didn't anticipate there also comes — frequently from the same people — a hatred I didn't anticipate either). Yet even today I don't think I can honestly say that I feel loved consistently, especially (again) since in addition to love/hate there comes love/exploit and the resulting "no good deed goes unpunished" syndrome. I'm afraid to trust love sometimes because I have learned how much ambivalence comes along with love. Well, I still take my chances, but I've learned to be wary.

Yet with all those qualifications it is still fair to say that I only intermittently feel that I am indeed the beloved child — or that You are my beloved spouse. I do all the sociological work on that imagery, but I don't experience it much myself. Now more than I used to but still not much.

The reasons are complicated and I'm sure go deep into my own past. It's a problem that will never be solved completely. Nonetheless, like Simon in the story, I must strive to be more open to love, Yours and others'. And to be, if not less wary, at least less suspicious.

And when I say, "I love You," as I do at the end of these reflections every day, I do mean it, however weakly and timidly and imperfectly.

October 3, 1993 — Chicago

My Love,

I must run because I have the 7:30 Mass at St. Mary's. I love You. Give me strength and confidence and courage and faith.

All of them? Well, why not ask for the moon. And the sun and the stars too.

October 4, 1993 — Chicago

My Love,

A shooting in Moscow this morning. "Diehard" Communists and nationalists resisting the end of their power. Not unlike the old guard in the Church (and the new papal encyclical) trying desperately to hang on to their power to dictate to the laity without listening to them. What folly!

Jack's tape yesterday was about Peter and forgiving seven times seventy times. Forgiveness is part of being a person. If one cuts off forgiveness, one cuts off contact with the flow of personhood and blocks the flow of forgiveness into the self. It is human to forgive, despite the dictum confining it to You.

So much hatred in the world. Ireland, Russia, Somalia, Israel. People consumed with hate and unable to forgive. Protect me from ever falling into that trap. And help me to contain the anger that so often surges within me. Perhaps there are reasons to be angry, but I must not permit it to dominate my life, a temptation that has always been serious for me and probably always will be.

I'm getting better at forgiveness. Help me to continue to improve so as not to cut off the flow of Your love and so that I'll really mean it when I end each day with "I love You."

October 5, 1993 — Fargo, N.D.

My Love,

Jack reminds me again in the tape I listened to yesterday that I cannot force the spiritual life by will. It's not so much doing certain things, though that of course is necessary too, but seeing things a certain way. The only way that the will enters in, it seems to me, is that you can at least discipline yourself to take time to see. As Jack says in the tape, it comes and it goes.

The most important thing to see is that I am the beloved child and that I live in a garden that You have given. Not a perfect garden, not one where I am always safe, not one where things can't go wrong, but still a lovely place. On this autumn day in North Dakota the sky is really *big!* — for which I ought to feel grateful and in which I ought to see You. This "ought" is not an obligation, only an opportunity.

I'll try to see You and Your opportunities in the rest of this crazy week. At least it won't be dull.

I love You.

October 15, 1993 — Chicago

My Love,

I pray for my friend whose marriage is in trouble. What a sad story and what little prospect for a happy ending. Maybe such an ending was possible a long time ago, but no more. What can be done for such people? One supports them the best one can and leaves the rest to You. It didn't have to be that way, but it is and with most of the Church's input being negative. They made their own decisions, sure, but I'm not sure they saw any options, or not very clearly. They once were in love, or at least thought they were, each of them perhaps wanting different things out of marriage and neither of them getting it, not fully anyway.

But You love them, and You will dry every tear. Moreover, You will give them the chance to work it out eventually one way or another.

As for me there is nothing I can do now but continue to be supportive as best I can. I am not You. My inclination to think that I can will happy or happier endings on people is foolish. Even You can't do that, at least not in the short run. What strange people we humans are, strange, strange people. In addition to our fear of finitude and death, we are so ignorant, so limited, so insensitive, so unaware. Not because of malice but because of finitude. We see our chances all too dimly. Well, realizing my own inability to make all things well and wipe away every tear (which is to say recognizing I am not You), I do what I can, pray, and leave the rest to You.

I'm full of a sense of my own limitations this morning, am I not, my Love? You're probably saying that it's about time!

I love You.

October 16, 1993 — Chicago

My Love,

Another dream last night about the seminary. I'm astonished at how many dreams I have about that place. I was head prefect in philosophy but as a theologian and responsible for a small group of seminarians. Such a terrible decline of vocations in a couple of years, I thought. I rushed around to meet deadlines just as I am rushing now. I didn't like the place any more now than I did then, but I still lamented for what it had become.

The dream came from a book I read part of yesterday and a conversation and the usual rushing and it was a highly creative combination of those events. Yet there was sorrow over what has happened to the so-called "confident Church" of forty years ago, done in by shallow intellectuals and foolish leaders. We are better off now on balance than we were then, but the costs have been high and they are going to get higher. Worse still, wonderful opportunities have been wasted.

All very sad, one more example of what I am reflecting on lately — my own limitations. I tried with all my might to make the transition smoother, as though I was You and was responsible for it and could do it myself. Well, perhaps I exaggerate, but surely You must have been amused by my frantic efforts. Which is not to say that they were not worth the effort.

I am again beset by feelings of failure like those I had a dozen years ago. Nothing I try seems to work. Of course that's silly, but I do feel I've been on the side of lost causes.

Nonetheless, one does what one can and leaves the rest to You.

I love You, by the way. Help me always to love You more.

October 17, 1993 — Chicago

My Love,

In Jack's tape he reflects on the story of the hairs of the head and the sparrows as a response to our fear of death. Fear not those who can kill the body, Your son says, but those who can destroy us utterly. The deepest fear is not of death but of non-being or existential isolation, of becoming nothing at all. One should fear that, He seems to be saying, if that were the way things were going to be. But it is a fear whose validity He rules out by saying that You have counted the hairs on our head and value us as individuals more than we can possibly imagine. We will continue to be afraid because both our lives and our being are in jeopardy, constant jeopardy, from both death and extinction. Death will conquer us, but we will not be extinguished. Death will conquer me, but I will not be extinguished because You know and care about me as a person. I believe that, though it's hard to live like that belief is driving my life because there is so little proof of it besides Your word as delivered in Jesus.

In truth we all have somewhere in the corner of our self the feeling that this might be true, that we might be loved, that we might in fact be "beloved children." So Jesus confirms a hunch we have in our best moments. I know it's true, but on this grim, rainy Sunday morning with so much to do and so many idiots all around, that belief does not penetrate my personality all that much. I'll keep trying to respond or, more appropriately, to accept the good news.

I love You.

October 19, 1993 — Chicago

My Love,

Jack's themes on the tape I listened to yesterday continue to be concerned with fear. Your son, from Mark 8 on, touches everyone whom he cures physically — taking on himself all their fear and anguish. His physical death was not a payment back to God, as our bad theology used to say; it was rather a going down into the depths of human suffering to show that You would be with us, even as You were with Your son, in the valley of death and in every other suffering that we could possibly know, even the suffering that comes from a sense of being abandoned by all that we thought loved us. You would be with us because we too are Your beloved children. At that level of reality we cannot be destroyed, cannot be abandoned, cannot die forever, cannot be cast into rubbish heaps.

Jesus even went into hell, according to some of the early creeds, because even there Your mercy cannot be excluded — an interesting theory given the Church's history of raging about hell. Yet, in fact, who are we to put limits and constraints on what Your mercy and Your love can do?

This is very powerful stuff — and very reassuring. Some of it begins to ooze into my personality, and that surely is an improvement. Please help me to believe more strongly and let that which I know to be true about Your love surge to my consciousness and shape my life.

I love You.

October 31, 1993 —

My Love,

First time in nine days. As You know (and I believe that, at the most, You tolerated it) my computer blew up a week ago Friday. I have brought Julie's machine home from the office and at least am able to work again and pray again after wasting a precious week.

Anyway I realize now how psychologically and spiritually dependent on these reflections I have become. They force me to concentrate on *You,* and I am very grateful for Your having given me the idea about this prayer form.

Tomorrow I'll be back, presumably on this computer.

I love You.

November 1993

❦

November 1, 1993 — Chicago

My Love,

Finally, after ten days the computer is working again, and my life is back in order. It's been a long time. Also I have bronchitis, which is a lot better than pneumonia, but I seem to be getting over it, however slowly.

I've been watching the TV series on the Great Depression, searching, I suppose, for some of my own identity. Last night two segments (Ford Motor, and Pretty Boy Floyd) were profoundly moving. I wept at some of it, thinking how much my parents and those of their generation suffered — and in the process made the world a much better place for us. Dear God, how does all this suffering and generosity work itself out? I realize that I'm asking for a calculus that only You can understand. I also understand my fury at those young punks who don't understand that era and don't care about the marks it has made on American society and on the souls of so many of us. I am glad I didn't have to live through those terrible years, save as a child, and I'm sorry my parents suffered so much and grateful to them for what they were able to pass on to me. Help me to understand and be grateful that I have stood on the shoulders of giants. I love You.

November 4, 1993 — Chicago

My Love,

I went to the Jesuit fund-raising party for their home for old priests last night. It was a classy, classy operation. The party was at the Merc club on South Wacker overlooking the river. The view of the river, illumined by lights, was fantastic. What a beautiful city. Thanks for making me a Chicagoan.

The Lady Margaret (Daley), as I call her, was one of the co-hosts, and she brought her husband along. I continue to marvel at his boyish enthusiasm, one of his most admirable traits. He particularly likes to offer people rides home in his cars. Again we're lucky in this city, for which many thanks.

The table I was at was all Christ the King people. How strong the ties! They still remember my work from thirty years ago, which I guess proves that I wasn't the failure there I thought I was. It still shocks me, however, that people I taught in grammar school have children that are adults now too! I guess I really am sixty-five.

One woman was astonished that I remembered her exact address after thirty years. But those sorts of things one never forgets.

Thanks too for those memories and for all the graces of that era of my life.

I love You.

November 5, 1993 — Chicago

My Love,

We went to the orchestra hall last night for a wondrous concert. Gould, Grieg, Copland, Respighi. Pure romanticism, of course, but lovely. Hard to choose among them. Morton Gould himself, at the age of eighty, was there, and seemed vigorous and very pleased with the applause. So much lovely music in his lifetime, not perhaps Mozart or Bartok, but a lot more pleasurable to a lot more people.

So much beauty in Your world, so very much. For it all I thank You.

I love You.

November 13, 1993 — Dublin

My love,

I just finished writing a column in defense of the Cardinal [Bernardin] which I will fax off to Chicago in hopes that it will appear somewhere next week. I'm sure that it will appear somewhere. I wish I were in Chicago to handle it myself, but You willed that I be there, and that settles that, doesn't it?

Please grant the Cardinal the strength to see hope in this terrible situation. Any priest in America can now be attacked in the same way, even by people he doesn't know or has never met. Evil is loose in the world as a result of the cover-up of the past, and we must pay the price. Dear God, what a terrible, terrible mess for a Church that doesn't need more mess.

I love You.

November 14, 1993 — Dublin

My Love,

A bright Sunday morning in Dublin, but I grow more discouraged about the attack on the Cardinal. Mary Maher remarked to me on the phone this morning that once a good cause emerges, it is never long before someone abuses it, especially when the media are willing to engage in a feeding frenzy. We are having a local one here in Ireland because one of the Sunday papers is publishing an interview with Eamonn Casey, a pathetic yet powerful interview. Poor Eamonn. Poor Joe. Poor everyone.

This business of trial by accusation is a terrible thing. Yet the first sexual abuse victims had no recourse but to go to the media, because the Church was not responsive.

So too causes for concern: the damage the Church has done to itself and now to the best bishop we have and the pernicious practice of feeding-frenzy conviction by accusation.

I was, as You remember, the victim of one such assault a dozen years ago (why do these things always happen when I'm out of the country and must run up a huge overseas phone bill!) and I know what it's like and how unfair it is.

I worry, worry, worry. It can be done to anyone, anyone. Evil rampant.

A very distinguished Chicago lawyer, maybe the best trial lawyer in the country, is willing to take on the defense of the Cardinal for free and to finish it in short order. I doubt that he can get through the wall of legal hangers-on around the Cardinal. I talked to the man last night and suggested that he work through Rich [Mayor Daley]. I don't have the clout to deliver that kind of link. Not from here anyway. Nor even if I flew back to Chicago.

If You would, please help the Cardinal to see this man and listen to him — and Rich to serve as the intermediary.

Now I'm off to Maynooth, which will be a haunting experience after all that is happening.

I love You.

November 15, 1993 — Dublin

My Love,

I continue to be dismayed by the ease with which a person's reputation can be destroyed by mere accusations, as the Cardinal's has been. It should be possible to clear his name rather quickly, but I'm not sure he has the legal talent to do that.

Right now I figure I have spent enough time and energy on the cause of sexual abuse by priests and will give up in disgust on what it has become. But that is a decision that I should not make while traveling.

I'm off now to get my printer fixed. Continue to help me during this trip. And, once more, I beg You to help the Cardinal.

November 16, 1993 — Dublin

My Love,

June said yesterday that she was glad I was not around for all the trouble in Chicago. I would certainly have been harassed by the media. Still I hope my column appears. The Cardinal is entitled to my support. Again I ask You to take care of him.

November 17, 1993 — Dublin,

My Love,

Last night I gave my lecture in Limerick on the Russian data. It was well received, though by its nature as sociology it was less entertaining than other talks I might have given. Still I think it was a wise decision to be a serious scholar this time.

I was up at 5:15 this morning after getting to bed late because of another call from America about the Bernardin crisis. He seems to be making his way through it pretty well, for which many thanks to You. I bet there's a huge increase in the Cardinal's Appeal contribution this year. It's an ill wind that doesn't blow some good.

I love You.

November 19, 1993 — Dublin

My Love,

I spent much of the day worrying about the American Airlines strike. I will probably get back to Chicago on Monday one way or another. I do have backup reservations, which at this stage of the game are terribly expensive and I'll use them only if the Delta backup that AA provides does not work. Rough strike. The cabin attendants are taking their rage out on the people who are traveling at Thanksgiving, which will not help either the union or the company (on which they depend for a living) in the long run. But management must share the blame because of their bull-headed obtuseness. However, it is people who suffer. In this case I may well be one of the people.

I'm dead tired now after two lectures in two days, though both were well received, and the Trinity one, which is the main reason for my coming, was particularly successful. The provost's wife is a Blackie fan, which was very nice indeed.

The news from Chicago is good. The suit against the Cardinal is falling apart; the Chicago media and people are rallying, and this could turn out to be his finest hour. For this I am very grateful indeed. Continue, I beg You, to take care of him and protect him.

I still wonder as this day comes to an end what I'm doing here and what is the point of this whole dubious venture.

I really do want to go home.

I love You.

November 22, 1993 — Over the North Atlantic

My Love,

On the way home. I see the light is blinking, which means my problem is that the batteries were not charged or at least not adequately. I want to get this done before the battery gives out.

You have taken good care of me on this trip, despite the fact that the Aer Lingus engines wouldn't start this morning. The AA flight did indeed leave Manchester and because my reservation was all fouled up they put me in first class — with an empty seat next to me! Can't beat that when one expects the worse.

A hint of things to come. Well, sometimes one expects the worst and it happens. But every time one expects the worst with every good reason and it doesn't happen I think that, even if an angel isn't directly responsible, it is nonetheless a hint of what is to come — even if it is random chance.

I look forward with some dread to all the crises I must deal with when I get home, but it will still be nice to be home. The trip was all in all a good trip as I said yesterday, and I thank You for the opportunity and for the goodness of it.

A lot better than a wooden-hulled sailing ship!

And please take care of all the good people who were so kind to me on my wanderings.

I love You.

November 23, 1993 — Chicago

My Love,

Back in Chicago and catching up. I spoke to the Cardinal last night. He was in good spirits, aware that the tide had turned and pleased (as well he might be) with his response. The problem with sexual abuse continues, but at least it is clear that some outrageous charges cannot be sustained. Still, what a mess we have made of it.

I will get back tomorrow to reflecting on Jack's material about St. Mark and the mystery of death.

I love You.

November 24, 1993 — Chicago

My Love,

As I prepare to go to Grand Beach for Thanksgiving and realize that it will be a sad and difficult time, I think of all the families who must endure tragedy at this time of the year and must wonder whether there is anything really to be thankful about. Fear, suffering, and death are no respecters of "holiday" times. I wish I could make such suffering go away for everyone (such as the mentally ill Serbians I saw on TV last night suffering because of the Western blockade). I want everyone to be as relatively untroubled as I am at this time of the year. But that is a wish to be You, isn't?

I must put up with the limitations of my life and of the human condition and trust that in the end You will make all manner of things well. You know what suffering is like; You must know. You must suffer with everyone who suffers this holiday week, as any parent suffers when a child is in pain. I find myself thinking this morning (up since three o'clock because of jet lag) of the added line, "if You are." But of course You are; how else could we be? Did You Yourself not walk into the valley of death with Jesus to face the horror of being cut off utterly so that we know You can suffer too? I don't believe that the reason for the Incarnation is that You wanted to show us that You could suffer, but rather that You *do* suffer. When the time comes for my own death agony, help me to cling to that reality.

And for faith in it, I give the greatest thanks of all.

And tell You how much I love You.

November 25, 1993, Thanksgiving Day — Grand Beach, Michigan

My Love,

A typical Thanksgiving day this morning — gray, cool, stark. Not unlike, I suppose, the kind of weather that the Pilgrims endured in New England in late November. But I thank You nonetheless for this reminder of our need for gratitude and for the opportunity to express my gratitude in a more formal way.

Jack comments on his tape that the last part of the Gospel of Mark is about exorcising fear. The young man was afraid, but he returned. Peter was afraid, but he returned. The women were afraid, but we know their story so they returned. Jesus was afraid, but he overcame his fear. You know fear, though how that happens is a mystery. However, parents do fear for their children even though they know they will be all right. Concern about children is a virtue, but You are all virtue. Therefore You are concerned. Another name for concern is fear. Perhaps it is fear that we will not make the most of the opportunities fear provides for us. In any case in and through Jesus we know that fear is not final; hope and love are both stronger than fear. For that revelation of Your love and that sign of hope I am most grateful. In a way it is an even richer gift than the gift of life, for it is a promise that life is stronger than death. That I do believe. Help me to believe it more strongly and live that belief a little better than I do.

And thank You too for my family and my friends, for those I love and who love me, for all the blessings and graces of my life and for the good things You have given me. Help me always to remember to say thank You.

November 28, 1993, First Sunday in Advent — Chicago

My Love,

First Sunday in Advent. Snow flurries, thick clouds, sunshine peeking through. Perfect Advent Sunday morning. I preached yesterday on the alarm-clock-like sound of the Gospels for this Sunday — an alarm ringing in the dark on a cold winter morning. That's what Advent is supposed to be. This is a graced time of the year, dense with liturgical and natural symbolism, and the graces ought not to be lost. I preached yesterday on lost opportunities: the Bulls fan who stormed out of the room right before that final minute of the last game of the championship and missed Michael's drive from one end of the floor to the other and then Paxon's magical last shot. So it is with us. We're so busy getting ready for Christmas that we have no time to get ready for Christmas. What a terrible waste. And I'm no better than anyone else, maybe a little worse because I know what the symbols mean and I still don't give myself over to them.

This year I'm going to try with Your help to do better. I have set up a retreat time the week before Christmas, allegedly to go to Grand Beach, but maybe only to pretend that and actually hide here. Moreover I have managed to clear the deck from most major work. Still it will be a busy time and I'll need Your help if I'm to prepare for Your son's once and future coming by reading the signs of the times. Help me at least to do a little better than last year.

I know that Your son is coming!

I love You — and Him too.

November 29, 1993 — Chicago

My Love,

Why do I have this strange fascination with military history, which brought me to the McClurg Court yesterday to see *Gettysburg*? The film was horribly realistic. One had to keep telling oneself that it was only a film to avoid nausea. As it was, Pickett's charge was as gruesome — and as thrilling — as anything I've ever seen in a film. Folly! Tragedy! The depths of human evil and violence.

Yet part of the nation's history, part of the nation's tragedy. And so many of the men in my stories have fought in the wars and come home not quite whole after them. I suppose war is on my mind because there has been so much of it in my lifetime, especially when I was a kid and because my generation fought in two wars and watched its children break away in a third. You can't tell the history of my generation — as I try to do in my fiction — and not be aware of the importance of war.

I don't know what to make of it or of human nature. Surely the best and the worst of human nature was to be seen at Gettysburg — courage, cowardice, brilliance, stupidity.

Not much spark of the divine, as one of the characters said, and himself Irish at that.

Yet You are a parent of all of the more than fifty thousand men who were killed or wounded in that battle. How

You must have suffered! What do You make of it? What do You make of us? Why do You permit us to continue?

I am endlessly puzzled by these matters and will never find a solution, I know. Yet I must continue to puzzle.

In any event I believe that all manner of things will be well, and I love You.

December 1993

December 2, 1993 — Chicago

My Love,

Kirkus Reviews appeared yesterday with a comment on last year's journal [*Sacraments of Love*]. Like reviews of the two previous journals it baffles me. I cannot see myself as the admirable person in this journal, that the reviewers see. I realize how often I stumble through these morning exercises with hardly any religious or spiritual feelings, without any spiritual reading, and with discouragement, self-pity, and weariness. The reviewers don't see that. On the occasional times I try to read the books, I'm turned off in disgust. I wonder if there is some kind of unperceived hypocrisy in what I write on these mornings. I do my best to exclude the thought that they might some day be published. Indeed the first two years I thought they were not going to be published, and the reaction of the reviewers was much like this latest.

If I am misleading people, I am sorry. You know that I do these reflections as a form of prayer. I did them first of all as an experiment in praying, and now I do them because I *have* to do them; the day is incomplete without them. My image of You isn't always clear. Sometimes You are a very distant reader — and occasionally far too intimate a lover, one who frightens me as well as delights me.

Maybe I don't think I'm worth loving. I don't think I present myself as worth loving in these reflections. Yet the kind readers seem to like me. All of this confuses me enormously. It is one thing to say that I know You love me despite all my flaws. It is quite another to say that You find traits that are appealing in me. You and others — though God (You should excuse the expression!) knows that it is not a unanimous decision!

Secretly of course I am pleased with the review (as well as baffled by it). What author isn't pleased when a reviewer likes his book, especially when the book is an intimate self-portrait! That confuses me even more. Anyway, I will go on writing these reflections and publishing them if people want to read them and trust in Your love to make up for my deficiencies.

I love You.

December 3, 1993 — Chicago

My Love,

There's a terrible new pedophile scandal in California — a ring of twelve Franciscan priests at a California seminary abusing scores of kids. Usual pattern: denial by the Franciscans for years despite parental charges, then, somewhat unusually, an independent commission. One more nail in the coffin of the priesthood and still nothing said by the priest organizations around the country. Ugly, vicious, sick, self-destructive.

Apparently the claim that there is another accuser against the Cardinal was, like so many other rumors in the survivor network, not true. I don't see how the case can stand up. Yet there is the conviction in that network that all accusers are telling the truth and all priests who are charged are lying. We've brought that horror on ourselves too.

As I've told You before, I'm sick of this stuff. Yet I guess I have to keep talking about it and writing about it for at least a while longer. I'm going on CBS on Monday about the California case because there's a chance I can defend the Cardinal. Yet there's not much more I can do to awaken the Church and my fellow priests. I've tried that for seven years and I've failed.

What an ugly, terrible mess. Yet it reveals the sickness in the priesthood, not so much the sickness of sexual abusers but the sickness of clerical culture. What an ignoble fall for a group of men once held in such high respect.

I'm revolted and disgusted and sad. I will not live to see a rehabilitation of the image of the priesthood, even if I live another quarter century.

Anyway, I pray for the priesthood and my fellow priests.

I love You.

December 5, 1993 — Chicago

My Love,

Last night was the dinner at the Q club honoring [Msgr.] George Higgins. Despite the fact that he is pushing eighty, George seems as bright as ever. My talk was a failure. I figured it would be an academic audience, university types, and so I did a scholarly talk about the Catholic social ethic and where it came from. It turned out that the audience was heavily clerical, and my talk was too abstract. So it goes.

Men like George and Bill Quinn and Bill McManus,

heroes of my youth, are still impressive priests, real pros at the priest business. They are aging now, as I will be soon, and we will not see their like again. What a shame.

December 6, 1993 — Chicago

My Love,

A busy morning — CBS TV interview, trip to the dentist, then to the post office, then to the store, then back here. I'm sneezing again. I hope that I am not getting another cold. Indeed, if it's all the same to You, grant that I am not getting a cold.

Now that last sentence is the kind I always wonder about. Why bother the Lord of Creation — or, as I would rather say now, the Lady of Creation — with such a trivial request? Moreover, if I am getting a cold it is because of another chance encounter with a virus and perhaps because of my low resistance. Why should You intervene in the ordinary workings out of such chances? But then why should You intervene in anything? As You know, I don't doubt Your Providence, but I don't quite get how it works. And I'm sure that we have yet to figure out how the question ought to be framed. The notion that nature and grace are in some kind of conflict still lurks in our theological unconscious.

Moreover, the San Francisco research shows that prayer does facilitate the recovery of those in cardiac care units. So prayer does work, somehow or the other, and You do want us to pray. So I feel free to pray with prayers of petition and I do so pray, though surely not often enough. I should go back to my old custom of praying at the end of the day for all those who need my prayers. I'll try to do that tonight. I don't know how I got out of the habit. Make a written list. I love You.

December 7, 1993 — Chicago

My Love,

Last night's supper at Rog Kaffer's was disconcerting. We went through a list of classmates who are either sick or dying. There are only three of us who are still active priests of the archdiocese (not including me). That's a terrible decline from the thirty-four who were ordained forty years this May.

Death, resignations, retirements, sickness. This I think is much higher than the rate for men our age. I don't understand it, especially the retirements, though perhaps if I were still in the parish priest game I would understand it better. Men get tired, especially men who were not prepared for the fantastic changes and crises. I have a big batch of names for my list of people for whom to pray.

I don't feel old, don't act old, don't even look old, mostly because of good health (for which many, many thanks), exercise, and an exciting, if busy, life.

But I'm as mortal as those who are dying and I should not forget that. Life is winding down to the last few years — though it may continue for a reasonably long time yet. I ought not to permit myself to be under the pressure I'm under.

Yet what would I stop?

I don't know. I reflect on it often, as You know, and decide in the end to continue what I'm doing.

Anyway, I pray for all the class, even though I am long since alienated from them and ask You to heal and help them.

I love You.

December 15, 1993 — Chicago

My Love,

Ellen Davis had a nice comment about You on her tape yesterday: God, she said, is an incurable romantic — despite His (sic) realistic appraisal of the nature of human nature. You are the kind of person who falls in love with a flawed spouse and continues to fall in love despite the obvious faults of the spouse. Romantic that I am, I construe that to be a tremendous compliment to You. I am delighted to ponder the possibility that, like me, You believe in eventual happy endings. A romance without illusion — that's a perfection if there ever was one, and I'm pleased to know that it is indeed one of Your perfections.

As the man says in the play about Gideon, there is no accounting for love. Why You should be a romantic about humans — and about me — is hard to fathom. But then I can't understand why so many people love me, yet they do, Yourself included. I don't feel very loveable this morning, but I must believe that I am because You Yourself have said so by creating me and sustaining me in existence. Help me to grow in my sense of Your incurable love this Christmas season.

Grant that there me some signs of hope in the Russian election mess. And that the peace proposal for Northern Ireland work.

Anyway, I love You. Help me to be as incurable a romantic as You are.

December 20, 1993 — Chicago

My Love,

I went walking last night about five o'clock, already dark as we approach the solstice. Michigan Avenue was filled with people. I found myself filled with love for all of them — see what happens when I slow down! I guess I can understand why You love us when I have that experience.

I still feel new and unconnected, trying to be born again, I suppose. I am confident that the rebirth will happen if I give it half a chance.

Guide me during these precious days.

I love You.

December 22, 1993 — Chicago

My Love,

I've been reflecting on my life and on the kind words some people have said about my life's work in recent years. George Higgins was so generous as to call me "a towering figure in the American church" at his honorary dinner. It's not true, of course. I'm a pariah, and that's that. And yet, a part of me knows that with Your help I have had an impact on American Catholicism and indeed on the world beyond the Church.

You designed me and my life for that purpose, a purpose that is still mysterious to me. It often seems that it almost doesn't matter what I do. You, as always playing it by ear, direct me to Your goals. I really ought to just give myself over to Your plans and not fight them. There's a thin line here between trust and passivity, and the name of the line, I think, is serenity and confidence in You.

I say this and I must come to believe it: if my life were to end tomorrow I would have done, however imperfectly, what You wanted me to. There is no more point in worrying about what comes next. Enough has come already. If You grant me life and health and the grace to follow Your lead (which sometimes is unbelievably subtle and obscure, though not in retrospect) the trajectories will perhaps continue.

From the point of view of eternity or even of a hundred years or even of ten years, to be a towering figure in the American Church is to be not very much at all. It is interesting to speculate on what one's obituary will look like — controversial popular novels ("steamy"), thin skin, controversial sociology, conflicts with bishops, three homes, etc., etc. Such an obit will miss much, but that is the way of the world. And fifty years from now what of my work will survive? Not all that much, if any at all. My life, my struggles, my hesitations and doubts, my fears and my gambles will be utterly forgotten.

So I've accomplished a lot in my life, much of it unplanned and a lot of it unconscious, but even that lot is not very much, indeed trivial. From the point of view of time, to say nothing of eternity, even "towering figures" are pygmies, and popular novels and original thought are dust.

But it does not follow that one should not always do one's best. A life's work is both nothing (or very little) and everything. It will not last, and yet it will last forever. The slightest influence for good on another human person will never die. It will be at least remembered always by that person and by You for all eternity. So nothing matters and everything matters. One must know who one is and where one comes from. One must perceive how relatively minor the very best, and that one does is and yet how it is also essential. One must therefore both care and not care. It is true for everyone.

There is no escaping from that paradox. To care means to work hard and do one's best not to care means to retain serenity and trust no matter what happens.

This is in part the reintegration, the rebirth, the ordering of chaos, the light of the star that I need at this

Christmastime, the sense of beginning again. I pray that it will make at least a little change in my life.

I am also grateful for this retreat interlude. Would that I could live this way all the time!

I love You.

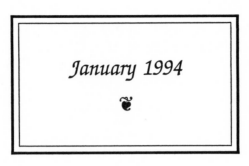

January 1994

January 1, 1994, New Year's Day
(Feast of Mary at Christmastime) — Chicago

My Love,

A warm and bright beginning of the New Year. Sunshine. Temperature near forty. It wouldn't be much better in Tucson, except for thirty degrees or so of temperature! May it be a good omen for the world and my family and myself.

I enjoyed the party last night, which makes it the first New Year's party I have enjoyed in a long time. The payoff from the retreat I made before Christmas continues. Why didn't I think of making these retreats more often?

I also hope that in Tucson some of the frantic rushing that has marked the time since Labor Day will diminish. I have suspended sociology till the spring quarter (save for copy editing of books) and will work only on my fiction and that, with Your help, at a slower and less frantic pace than in the past.

I was thinking last night of how often I have stood in the way of the work You want me to do for others. My own personal agenda has often been at odds with what I see in retrospect was Your agenda. My fears and insecurities have blocked Your goals. My anger has interfered with

Your love. I can't help but feel that my life is deeply flawed, defensive when it should have been confident, hassled when it should have been serene, weary when it should have been joyful. Help me to more of those latter adjectives in this year that is starting today.

Last night I heard a nice example of the sort of thing that bothers me. I was talking to two people. The man turned to the woman and said, "See, he *is* friendly. What they told us isn't true."

What had *they* said about me? It turned out that the advance billing was that I was distant and reserved.

Now, You know me well enough to know that I'm neither, that indeed I couldn't be distant or reserved even if I tried. Even when I don't enjoy parties (which is usually) I am just the way I was last night because that's the way priests should be. Why would anyone feel the need to lie about me?

No, the proper question is, Why do I feel the need to be upset about it after all these years? I laughed it off last night and am not bothered this morning. It goes with the territory, and it tells more about others than it does about me. But help me to live that way during the new year.

I love You.

January 2, 1994 — Chicago

My Love,

Yesterday I put away all the Christmas stuff — lights, trees, cribs (seven of them — what do you give to a priest for Christmas anyway?). It's always a sad experience, as is listening to the last Christmas music on the audio in my car. Such a bright, shining season and it passes so quickly. I can't claim that my Christmas was any more mystical than last year, but at least it was more pleasant, and I was

in a better and happier mood because of the retreat I made
the week before, an experience I intend to repeat at least
three times during the course of the year — Easter and
June would be the other two.

So I'm sad to see Christmas end but also glad that the
eating is over for a while. I hate the sight of food and know
that I must fast for a time if only for health purposes —
which may have been a point in the fasting rules from the
start. Anyway, whatever the mixed motives for fasting they
can be directed toward self-control, which is a grand idea,
as the Irish would say.

Time slips by now so quickly, the complaint of everyone over twenty-one, though I suspect that the complaint
becomes more poignant — and more terrified — with the
passage of the years. Whether I am in late middle age (as
I would like to think and my general health suggests) or
in old age (as my coming birthday indicates), the truth remains that the years are running down. I must not deceive
myself about that. On the other hand, living in morbid
fear is silly if understandable. One must live as best one
can with as much vigor and hope and generosity as is
available. And above all with the sense that one is loved.

By You.

An unpredictable, vulnerable, willful, implacable, difficult, and tender lover.

Who knows what She's doing, even if I don't.

How else can it be with love?

And I do love You.

January 3, 1994 — Chicago

My Love,

We saw *Ruby in Paradise* yesterday at Roger Ebert's suggestion. It certainly was one of the ten best films of the

year, a story of "initiation" — a young woman's beginning to discover who she is and what life means. She will
certainly have to come to terms with her fundamentalist
upbringing, which is a good deal more difficult than to
come to terms with a Catholic upbringing because, even
at its worst and despite the efforts of parents and priests
and nuns, still has enough streams of pluralism creeping
in that alternative Catholicisms are always available.

Yet I couldn't help reflect on how much more difficult
Ruby's task was than mine and that of the young women
of my generation. We lacked mobility and we grew up surrounded by acceptable paradigms from which we could
choose. We didn't have to work it out all by ourselves
as she did, and our paradigms were flexible enough to
change and grow and we changed and grew as the Church
(quite unexpectedly) changed.

Was it better for Ruby, if not easier? God shapes the
back to fit the burden, as my mother used to quote the old
Irish saying. There was still the need even for us to work
out what life meant on our own, even if it was not as difficult as Ruby's task. We were also in process too (and still
are). Yet it was and is easier for those who are part of a
tradition within which they are able to live and move and
think and grow, which is what Catholicism, even of the
1930s, West-Side variety, was and is.

I marvel today at how fed up I am with the Pope and
the hierarchy and most of my fellow priests, a state of
mind that would have seemed improbable forty-five years
ago, but not absolutely impossible. Yet my loyalty to the
heritage and the tradition is stronger than ever. I thank
You for both the flexibility and resiliency of my heritage.

And I deplore the prejudice against Notre Dame that
led both the coaches and the sports writers to pass them
over for number 1 yesterday!

I'm off to Tucson in thirty-five minutes. Protect me on

the trip and while I'm out there and protect all those I love
in my absence.

I love You.

January 6, 1994 — Tucson

My Love,

I read Robert Lowell's poem last night that asserts that
You are not dumb, i.e., mute, a contention that may very
well amuse You. His point, as You know since You have
doubtless read the poem too, is that revelation did not
end with the Bible but that it continues as each generation
writes the stories of its insights and wisdom. Yes, we take
our wisdom wherever we can find it. We listen desperately
for Your voice wherever there is a chance that we may hear
it. We search for Your presence in all the daily events of
our life. If one believes that creation is a sacrament of Your
loving presence, then one must seek sacraments wherever
they may appear.

I love You.

January 7, 1994 — Tucson

My Love,

I read the first chapter in John B. Keane's *Messages to the
Brain* yesterday, a message from his stomach. It was hilar-
iously funny but also made a good point about how much
we depend on our bodies and how badly we treat them.
You were remarkably ingenious in devising the human organism (though a long evolutionary process). While there
are some apparent mistakes (the suffering of women at
childbirth, the need for less food as we grow older with
no matching decline in appetite), it is not my intention

to argue about the details of design. The human organism does pretty well what it is supposed to do: reproduce and expand culture. I suppose its biggest weakness is fear, which leads to most of the horrible things we do to other people — from the attack on skater Nancy Kerrigan yesterday to the Serbs celebrating Christmas by killing as many Bosnians as they could.

The stomach is a particularly marvelous organ and, as Keane argues, we tend to use it badly by eating and drinking too much. While I am not the offender he claims to be in his story, I have clearly been eating too much these past several months, especially when I'm traveling. I at least don't abuse the "creature" all that much.

So I'm grateful to You for my stomach and all my other organs and for the wisdom with which You have produced our bodies, and I promise to take good care of mine in the years that remain to me.

I also read some of the poems by Barbara Sigmund that Cokie Roberts (her sister, as You know) sent to me. They represented the even more ingenious dimension of the human organism, its courage in the face of tragedy, a courage that does not pretend the tragedy isn't there. Grant that I may react with such courage when my life is in jeopardy, neither denying or running from it.

I love You.

January 8, 1994 — Tucson

My Love,

Like Mechtilde of Magdeburg Barbara Sigmund found some kind of light in the pain of the cancer that racked her poor body. I think of all the people I know who are suffering physically and wonder if I could see light in such suffering, much less be as brave as they are. Dear Love, help me in the times of suffering and crisis that are surely ahead of me in my life.

January 9, 1994 — Tucson

My Love,

There has been much about light in my reading the last couple of days; it has a powerful impact on me because of the brightness of Tucson this January. I love darkness too, as You well know, particularly and oddly Dublin darkness in November. But I have a hard time with dark nights and endless gray days, which is Chicago during winter and much of spring. My Love, let Your light shine on me for the rest of my life. I love You.

January 14, 1994 — Tucson

My Love,

Jack Rosenthal, the once and again editor of the *New York Times* magazine, called me yesterday to ask me to write an article on why I am still a Catholic — a great challenge and a great opportunity. As I thought about the piece an enormous amount of anger welled up in me at the idiots who run our Church and the tremendous harm they have done in the last forty years. It will be necessary to express that anger in the article, though I must do it carefully so as not to sound like I have sour grapes, especially since Jack wants the article to be personal. The bottom line is that I like being a priest and I like being Catholic regardless. Moreover, that's the way the laity react too. There is the key problem in the piece: how to explain why the laity like being Catholic despite the fools who govern the Church.

This will be a difficult and an important piece and I must do it right. Help me to carry it off well. I really mean that: often I feel that someone is whispering in my ear when I write. I realize that it is my own preconscious, but I believe You work through all creation and hence that You are at work through my preconscious. I must listen carefully to what I hear You saying. I beg You to help me say what You would have me say.

January 17, 1994 — Tucson

My Love,
The mystic Ruysbroeck in the meditation I read last night speaks of three offers of love from You. The first is in the beauty of creative things, the second is in friends and people who love us, the third is in death.

That's an arresting thought — death as an offer of love. But if one believes in You that's just what death is — the beginning of a life of exciting love. I do believe in that vision, sometimes more than others. So I must look to death as a renewal of love and try to prepare for it as best I can by accepting with calm confidence the death interludes that attack me through my life. It isn't easy. Maybe I'm a little better at it than I used to be, but I have a long way to go.

Please help me. I love You.

January 18, 1994 — Tucson

My Love,
Please take care of all my friends who are ill, especially Jack Durkin and Jim Coleman.

I love You.

January 20, 1994 — Tucson

My Love,

Writing the new novel has been a lot of fun. The protagonist is an eccentric genius at nineteen who does not want to accept his abilities and denies them to himself, but at the same time does things that are certain to showcase his odd abilities, a man doomed to be great despite his own intentions and wishes and hence necessarily a comic figure. In past versions, people have been unable to figure him out. He's a complex character but not so unusual that there are not others like him. The difference between him and a lot of real people I know is that he does not finally reject his genius. He is forced to accept it by the women around him and by his own compulsively quick tongue. I think the story holds together as a complex plot, but I think some people will be uneasy about the lead character — publisher and editors for example. Well, I must write what I want to write and let others worry about it. I find my stories becoming more picaresque. Bad enough that they be religious, I guess. But how can I write about Irish men and not have picaresque characters?

Anyway, I thank You for the fun that comes from writing novels. I am grateful to You that I have been less compulsive about this one.

January 27, 1994 — Tucson

My Love,

I've been doing some analysis on the *L.A. Times* priest study and the news is very good indeed — at least in some respects. Most priests would become priests again if they had it to do all over; most say the priestly life is better than they expected; almost all say they will not leave;

and only a rather small proportion say that they would marry if they could. Moreover, these findings are not fundamentally affected by age. So the alleged morale crisis doesn't exist (except among about a quarter of those who describe themselves as liberal), and celibacy is clearly not the problem that it is made out to be for most priests.

The state of clerical culture now is such that many priests will bitterly deny the findings. They may like being a priest, they will insist, but most of the guys are not happy. This pluralistic ignorance, I am convinced, is at the heart of the vocation crisis. Priests don't recruit young men because they *think* that so many of their colleagues are unhappy. Yet the priesthood is one of the happiest groups of men in the country. There ought to be a way to break out of this swamp of pluralistic ignorance, but I'm not sure yet what it is. We'll have the vocation crisis half-way beaten. The other half is more realism about the plusses and minuses of marriage. More people leave their marriages or are thinking of doing so than leave the priesthood.

I think it can be done. I'm having supper with the Cardinal next Wednesday, and I'll try to get him thinking seriously about it. It's the first breakthrough opportunity I've seen in a long time.

Help us to make something good out of it.

I love You.

January 29, 1994 — En route to Chicago

My Love,

I have a wonderful idea for a new science fiction novel to be called *Angel Friend* about the angel Raefaella, the younger sister of my Gabriella from *Angel Friend*. I propose to tell the Tobias story again, but make Toby Shannon, my hero, a computer hacker and a nerd. He will establish contact with Rae, as she calls herself, on Internet. It will turn out that angels eavesdrop on Internet all the time and that it is possible if you know the right code to get through to them. The point will be utterly theological: angels are Your representatives in taking care of us and thus revealing Your love for us as individual persons. You will be referred to by Rae as "The Other" and Your son as "The One."

It sounds like great fun. I'll write it even if there is no immediate contract for it. I hope You like it.

I love You.

February 3, 1994 — Chicago

My Love,

I feel, old, tired, battered, exhausted. Give me strength please for the rest of the week and bring me back safely to Tucson and a little peace.

All I can do this morning is to cry out in dismay. Please help me. I love You.

February 5, 1994 — Chicago

My Love,

Sixty-six-years old, my Love! That's a long time. How many more birthdays? That's for You to say, not for me. I'll accept however many there are, many or few. Sometimes during this crazy week of rushing with so many things to do and so little time, I've actually found myself thinking that death would be a kind of relief from the frantic rushing to keep up with obligations, responsibilities, hassles, and worries. It's pretty bad when one begins to think that way, but this week has been absolutely hellish, even worse than I had expected, and I expected something pretty bad.

127

One thing is for sure: if life continues like it did this week, there will be very few birthdays.

Strange thoughts for a birthday, aren't they? No feeling of celebration at all. Just a desire to get out of town tomorrow morning. Terrible.

But I must express my gratitude despite all the problems and the hassles of this time in my life. I am grateful for life itself, for all the loves, and the family and the friends and for the excitement and the opportunity and the challenges and for Your love and support and comfort and all the other good things that have happened in my life.

Despite this week from hell, mine has been a very fortunate life indeed. If I have problems just now, the reason is that I've been trying to do so many things and that it's all catching up with me finally. How many times have I said I must rearrange my life and have failed to do so? This week is proof again that I must do so, but there is no clear way out that I can see. Help me to see it.

I love You. I really do, and I am deeply grateful for life and for its gifts. Please excuse my complaints on what should be a happy birthday. Help me, too, to at least seem happy tonight at the party.

February 8, 1994 — Tucson

My Love,

What a terrible mess I made of things last week. I don't mean the pressures or even the way I responded to them. I mean rather my lack of reflection, of awareness, of sensitivity to Your presence all around me. I let myself be rushed to the point of distraction. Never once did I say to myself, "Now, hold it. What's going on here? What am I about?"

I lost track of You and Your love and what I'm supposed to be. After almost a half century of struggling with the spiritual life I am almost as inept at it as when I began. I cannot detach myself, even momentarily, from the rush of ordinary life to look at the world around me through the "third eye" — the eye of the spirit.

Well, the only response possible is that I must try again. Start over anew.

Help me to begin again. I acknowledge my terrible weaknesses in the life of Your Spirit. Help me to overcome at least some of it and be more aware of You as the day goes on.

Nonetheless, I know You still love me. And I love You.

February 14, 1994, St. Valentine's Day — Tucson

My Love,

The feast of romantic love, a phenomenon the Church does not seem to understand, though it is our feast. The problem is whether the word "love" as predicated of the human love we celebrate today is equivocal when it is predicated of You. In principle the Church would deny that it is, but when it is finished explaining that analogy, the predication is virtually equivocal. Thus students simply reject the notion that there is any similarity at all between the love they experience and Your love for us — this despite the Song of Songs, St. Paul, and Your son. Indeed they are offended at the suggestion that human love might be a metaphor for divine love. They are completely different things, I am told. The notion that Your passion for us might be reflected poorly by the metaphor because of defect, because Your passion is so much more powerful than that of the most aroused lover, does not make sense at all.

Remember the woman at the focus group last year who was so repelled by the comparison? Clearly there had been something wrong in her sexual relationship with her husband, whether his problem or hers or a combination thereof is not to the point. We celebrate romantic love, powerful human passion, today but we are also afraid of it. When we link it with You, we expose ourselves to danger, it would seem. Are You really enthralled with us, are You really hungry for us, are You really aroused by us?

I think that, even conceding the necessity of the second element of the metaphor ("like but not like") we have to answer yes to those questions, or the analogy collapses altogether. So skittish is the Church when it comes to sexual pleasure that it has never really faced the full power of the metaphor. It's time that we do, isn't it?

So I have to assume (with all due regard for the metaphorical nature of the comparison) that I am Your Valentine, that You love me passionately, that You want me totally like a man wants his woman or a woman wants her man.

That is scary and I'm sure I won't think of it too long. Yet for a time today I should revel in it.

I return Your love as best I can.

February 15, 1994 — Berkeley

My Love,

There was a fascinating TV clip on Sunday night. The couple that was married in *Schindler's List* (which I hope to see tomorrow night when I get home) were celebrating their fiftieth wedding anniversary on St. Valentine's eve. The woman was apparently in bad health, her husband not so bad. But they both seemed very happy, valentines to each other indeed. Fifty years of happiness that were pure grace. Of course all happiness in this world is grace, but that one is extra special grace.

Could You love that man and that woman any less than they loved each other? Yet they would wish that their love would never end. So too must You. Any God worth the name would preserve that love. Perhaps the issue isn't so much why there is anything at all as why there is love. If there is love, does not there have to be Love?

I may, according to my dentist, have to undergo some kind of surgery to eliminate a cyst in my gums. Not a tumor, he says, and nothing to worry about, but I don't like the idea of anyone messing with my sinuses and that area of my skull. I am skeptical about it all and will undergo the surgery only if everyone (including my M.D.) says I have to. Of course it may not be necessary. I accept whatever is Your will, but I pray that it won't be necessary.

I love You.

February 18, 1994 — Tucson

My Love,

Not much praying these days despite my good intentions. So tied down by human weaknesses and demands on my time. No time for love. Sorry. I'll keep trying.

I love You.

February 22, 1994 — St. Petersburg

My Love,

My talk last night went well, though I realized as I was giving it that it could have been better organized and edited. Nonetheless I am not sufficiently witty and sufficiently skilled as a speaker to be able to get away with a paper that is less than perfect. It served its purpose for the meeting. I must, however, redo and edit some of the other papers on which I have worked during the past hurried weeks.

I spent a lot of time yesterday with students. I'm still able to relate to them. I feel a certain sadness about leaving here (though I will be happy to be home in Tucson at midnight) because I am a good teacher and good with students and yet I've never really been part of a campus community. However, after the disastrous effects of my Christ the King efforts at community, maybe that's just as well. Anyway, I am not about to question the trajectories that You have given to my life. It doesn't do any good, does it?

Today is the day Jack and my sister learn about the plans to deal with the cancer that is limited to the surface of his brain — as I remember it, an easier kind to eradicate. Help them, give them strength and wisdom, I beg You.

I haven't thought much about You during these times. Some but not much.

Help me to do better today.

I love You.

February 22, 1994 — Tampa Airport

My Love,

I hate conferences, hate 'em, hate 'em, hate 'em. Especially now that I'm worn out and have a long wait before I get home. You did not design my physiology for this kind of travel. However, I did it as a favor, and as Chicago Irish, I know what that means.

I've phoned Chicago a couple of times to find out about, Jack but no one is home. I'll try again before we board and then try them from Dallas if I have more time than I did on the way out.

As evidence of how clumsy I am in this state, I just knocked over a container of Pepsi, one that I had been very careful *not* to turn over.

Anyway, I love You and I'm grateful for all the advantages You have given me and for the graces with which You have blessed me.

Bring me home safely tonight

February 25, 1994 — Tucson

My Love,
Take care of Jack, please.
I love You.

February 27, 1994 — Tucson

My Love,
Joe Fichter died a couple of days ago. May You grant him peace and rest. He was my hero as a priest-sociologist, he the first of the empiricists and I the last of them. Not much of a dynasty, is it? I'm a relic of a former era, an era when professional competence as a priest was something to be admired and praised. Well, the concept was right and it will return eventually when the romanticism of the last quarter century is swept away.

I regret that after all the trouble blew over between us that I did not seek him out and try a reconciliation. But we didn't cross paths and I forgot about the troubles and forgot about Joe, save when one of his books came out. I remember praising the book on the Catholic charismatics. I didn't read the one on wives of priests.

I did not so much hold a grudge — I felt no ill will for years — as forget about my one-time hero. I'm ashamed of myself. I have reconciled with a lot of people, and I simply forgot about Joe until I read the obituary. Perhaps in Your world to come we can straighten things out. It does remind me of one more task, however which I must do with the next mail dictation.

It also looks like the charges against the Cardinal are being dropped tomorrow. I sure hope so. I wonder if CNN will give that the same publicity they gave the original charges. Not very likely.

I love You. Help me to continue to grow in wisdom.

February 28, 1994 — Tucson

My Love,

No word yet on the dismissal of the charges against the Cardinal. I assume that, as usual, news of innocence will travel less rapidly than news of charges.

Jack Durkin is going home today. I hope and pray that the treatment works.

I'll try to keep in contact with You during what could be a momentous and busy day.

I love You.

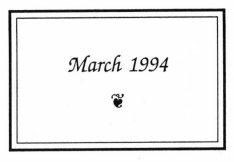

March 1994

March 1, 1994 — Tucson

My Love,

I slept only an hour and a half last night, overstimulated from all the things that happened yesterday — the exoneration of the Cardinal, two publishers wanting my book on Catholics and sex, commissioning of the article by the *New York Times*, a huge stack of mail. Unfortunately tonight is the annual party for me at El Charro, and I'll be a basket case if I don't get some sleep during the day.

Joe [Cardinal Bernardin] called me after his press conference (which was very successful) to thank me for the support and help. We've come a long way in a little over two years, for which many thanks indeed.

I hope this is a turning point in the pedophile problem, but it probably won't be.

I wrote my column about the unlucky innocents who don't have all the support the Cardinal did.

I am so tired now, my Love. Forgive my weariness. Help Jack Durkin.

I love You.

March 9, 1994 — Tucson

My Love,

This has not been a good week. First the fever, then the dental splint and a nasty chapped lip. I think I will have to fly back to Chicago tomorrow to see the dentist. The splint is too fragile to risk it being knocked out by someone not familiar with it. I'm kind of a basket case of aches and pains and frustrations.

I also want to pray for Jack and all the Durkins. I think its the beginning of the end for him now. Their problems are so much worse than mine. Please help them.

I love You. Help me to love You more.

March 10, 1994 — Tucson

My Love,

My mouth is a total disaster.

I love You.

March 12, 1994 — Tucson

My Love,

I'm better today but dragged out still from the trip and the three hours in the dentist chair. Some pain in my mouth but not much. No fever. Maybe cold coming on. All I need.

Thanks for providing me with the high quality dental help that I have and for returning my health, well, part way at least.

I love You.

March 21, 1994 — Tucson

My Love,

In my reading this morning St. Teresa talks about the soul being the castle, one might almost say the magic castle where one meets You. That is an interesting metaphor even if one can accept all the details of her interpretation. You lurk in the "soul" — the real self. To explore the real self is to go into the castle where You live and to discover You and Your glories. Fascinating! To know the self is to know God. That's the way it should be because the self is an image of You.

How little I know of You. How little I know of my self. How little I know of the castle within. Maybe in the few days left out here this week I can begin to explore the castle a little more and perhaps to write more poetry. I dedicate this retreat, as imperfect as it is, to You.

I love You.

March 22, 1994 — Tucson

My Love,

I continue to reflect on how little I explore my own interior castle, which is one of the places I can encounter You. It's not that I don't want to or not that I don't value the possibility. The reason is rather that I'm just too busy. Day after day after day I'm on the run. I think of You on occasion, but before I know it the day is over and I'm exhausted and I collapse into bed — another day of pointless rushing. And it will be worse when I get back to Chicago.

I try, You know I try. But my heart is not in my efforts, not really, because my heart is in my frantic attempt to keep up with all the demands of life, pseudo-demands I should call them.

To be able to reflect effectively, I need time and quiet, and neither of these are easy to come by. I'm beginning to wonder whether the retreat idea, which was so helpful to me at Christmastime, should be converted into one special day of prayer every month, back to the old day of recollection that marked my early years in the priesthood. It's a mechanical notion, but there's nothing wrong with mechanics as I stumble along the road into the castle where I hope to meet You. The first Sunday of each month perhaps?

It's worth a try.

I look at the calendar. The first Sunday of April is Easter, and I'll be on the move all day, though perhaps I could do it on Holy Saturday. The First Sunday of May I'm in Milano, but that might not be a bad place to reflect, if I'm awake.

Well, I'll try it, and I beg You for Your help.

I love You. Help me to know and love You better.

March 24, 1994 — Tucson

My Love,

I was very sleepy yesterday, a phase I suppose I had to go through as I started the retreat. I managed to read Rosemary Haughton's *The Catholic Thing*, which was a very good way to start a retreat even if one is sleepy. The Catholic "thing" she says, in summary, is to love everything in the world so much that the world is transmuted into heaven. It will never be a successful "thing" because our love is so imperfect, but it is our goal nonetheless and our imperfections will finally be made up by Your love.

Her position is something like my article for the *New York Times*. Catholicism needs both Mother Church and

Lady Wisdom, but the latter is more important though the former is absolutely necessary. Catholicism is not to be identified totally with the institutional Church, though the institution is necessary.

These days, with so much weariness when it is so hard just to keep going, I find that in the absence of energy the spiritual quest is hard to sustain. How do I explore the castle when I can hardly keep my eyes open?

The answer is that I must keep trying as long as I can breathe and walk and talk and You'll make up for my imperfections. You love me even when I'm tired, as all proper lovers do.

So I'll do my best with this retreat despite my weariness, and I will not consider it a failure just because I've been tired through the four days.

I love You, my love. Help me to love You more. Help me in this retreat.

March 26, 1994 — Tucson

My Love,

Last day in Tucson. I finally come out of the torpor that has bugged me through this retreat. It was of course the medicine I was taking. I don't know why I didn't think of that before.

As for the retreat, it has been good and despite the torpor I am convinced that (a) You love me and (b) there is nothing to fear. I can't promise to live in the wisdom of those two insights all the time, but I am still convinced and am eager for the Holy Week services to reenforce those beliefs. Again it won't be a perfect Holy Week, but it will be a better one because of this retreat.

I love You. I thank You for the blessings of these last three months and for the graces of the retreat. Bring me

home safely to Chicago and protect me during the next
two months.

March 28, 1994 — Chicago

My Love,

Back home on a typical gray Chicago March day. I've
been to the dentist already and my gums seem to have
improved, for which many thanks. I'm using today to get
organized.

I think I was all wrong recently when I was trying to
figure out why I don't feel grief more. As I was walking home from the dentist an ambulance went by, wailing
away. I thought of the person in it and of the suffering and
then of the family, mostly because I was in a reflective (or
possibly sleepy) mood. I almost broke down at the thought
of their pain. So I mourn all right — for all that suffering.
I try to control it because otherwise my mourning would
paralyze me completely.

It makes me think of how much You must suffer for
Your beloved children. The Italian woman in the *Times* this
morning, for example, single mother in her late twenties,
struggling to take care of the child and with an "angel dust habit." Plowed into a car and killed two Greek
priests. Held on Rikers Island on a murder charge. Almost
as destroyed as the two priests. How she suffers. How
much You suffer with her.

I can't cope with much less understand all this suffering. Holy Week is a fine time to reflect on it all, but still the
meaning escapes me completely. I will never understand
the meaning in this life, but I know that You care and suffer with us and that eventually You will wipe away all the
tears and all will be well, all manner of things will be well.

If that is not true then there is nothing to believe in. I

believe that it is true, yet I am still awed by the magnitude of human suffering.

Since I believe You are a parent, I think of You as a vulnerable God who "needs" to be consoled by your love children.

And I do love You and want to console You.

March 29, 1994 — Chicago

My Love,

I continue to be astonished by the short stories in Louise Erdrich's collection. It is absolutely unique. I am astonished that there are so many magical, grace-full stories written each year and even more astonished that they generally do not show up in the annual collections, unless someone with Louise's somewhat wild combination of magic and grace happens to be doing the collection.

There are sensibilities that are open to the magical and graceful dimension of reality, sacramental sensibilities I suppose one should say. I think I have that capability but I rush through life so quickly that there is never time to catch those moments. If only I could make more time for poetry and short stories, my religious and literary life would be so much better.

Once I get the Russian paper revised I will pull out of the sociological game for the next six months and try to return to the literary game. I've let it go too long, perhaps because of discouragement.

It's nice being back in Chicago. Nice, but cold. Help me during the chaotic six weeks between now and my return from Tel Aviv.

I love You.

April 1994

April 1, 1994 — Good Friday Chicago

My Love,

The Holy Thursday services last night at St. Mary of the Woods were wonderful. Just right. Leo's idea of washing hands instead of feet — teens washing, parish staff drying — is marvelous. Leo [Mahon] deserves more of the Church than he has received. He surely ought to be a bishop, not for his good but for the good of the Church.

I was deeply moved by the service, especially the *Pange Lingua* — the best of the old tradition combined with the new. The Catholic imagination at its best. And the reason why people remain Catholic. Why can't we do more of that? We must surely rescue the liturgy from the liturgists and the religious educators who have especially messed up the Easter Vigil by making it over two hours long. They love to keep people in church and bore them. Fanatics! Even worse, rubricists!

I'll be rushing all day, as I have said, but I must try to keep in mind that this is the day on which You showed us through Jesus that You would go down into the valley of death with us, so great was Your love. That is a love that I must keep in mind as I rush through the day. You are with me through the minor sufferings of this busy day just as

You were with Jesus on the major sufferings of the first Good Friday.

More time all day tomorrow. I love You.

April 2, 1994 — Chicago

My Love,

Please take care of Jack and all the Durkins.

I love You.

April 4, 1994 — Chicago

My Love,

Please help Jack and my sister and their beautiful family. And thanks for Easter and all the good things that reveal Your presence in the world.

April 5, 1994 — Chicago

My Love,

I went up to the hospital after supper last night. It was a terribly dispiriting experience, though what else would it be? Everyone is discouraged, tired, puzzled. How long will it last? How long can they take it? Help them, please.

There are no good ways to die. And, as Harry Petrakis said on the phone yesterday, so many prayers going up to You from all over the world that are not heard. I believe that all prayers are heard, but You grant only some of them because that's all You can do. I try to place the mystery there rather than in the assumption that You could hear all the prayers but do not do so for reasons of Your own. Bafflement all around. From Your point of view it all doubtless makes sense, and You suffer with and will take care of Your children somehow, some way, some day.

I am struggling with the mad rush to catch up that has affected me for the last ten days. I must let it go today.

April 5, 1994 — Chicago

My spiritual life has once again collapsed. Help me to pray better and more often and to be aware of Your presence in the world even on a gray, bland, dull Chicago day like this one. Help me to love You and live my life in the power of that love.

And in the faith that You will take care of us all, no matter what happens. I love You and I know that like so many of the heroines in my story You need and want my love. I'm sorry You have received so little of it these past few days.

April 6, 1994 — Chicago

My Love,

I found myself reflecting yesterday on the tragedy of individual deaths. The lawyer who took me to the Bulls game told me about a case in which a woman died because of the incompetence of a resident M.D. Not malice, but incompetence. I thought also of the young American who went to South Africa to work for the blacks and was killed by some black teenagers because she was white, despite her pleas for her life. The killers managed to avoid prosecution too, which may say something about what the future of South Africa will be like.

These two women deserved to live and yet died in final moments of terror because of stupidity in one case and hatred in another. Two individuals. Then I think of all the men and women killed in Bosnia and in the Zulu riots in South Africa and in the Holocaust, and I shudder in horror and anger and fear, especially when I try to get inside the imaginations of those who are about to die in such violence and feel their terror.

I'm sure You feel it too and suffer as they suffer. You feel it more acutely than I do because I'm able to turn off the experience and You are not. If You could stop such suffering, I'm sure You would. As to why You cannot, I do not know, save perhaps that You are locked in by the fact that You made rational creatures that are mortal and free. We all die, whether by mistake or hatred or merely the deterioration of our organisms. Mortality is the final problem. It is not merely wrong that a young woman should die; it is wrong that anyone should die. None of us has any guarantee of longevity or of graceful or peaceful deaths.

Your mistake, to put it that way, was to make rational creatures with whom You would fall in love and who were mortal.

The answer to the mistake is what we celebrate at this time of the year: we are not mortal after all. I think of Your son's metaphor about the woman in labor. I do believe that. I hope I will believe it myself when it comes my turn.

I love You. Help me to love You more. Please take care of all the Durkins for me and of all those poor people who will die today.

April 7, 1994 — Chicago

My Love,

The doctor told the Durkins yesterday that Jack is dying and has perhaps six weeks to live. I suppose we all knew it was happening. Yet it is different when you hear it in so many words and say it to yourself and others. They are doing pretty well, very Irish Catholic in their attitude toward death, assisted by Jack's wit.

Their kids are a credit to both of them, and they are doing well in the crisis. Poor, dear family, what a long time of strain and worry. It is good for everyone that they now see the end in sight.

More mystery to reflect on, more puzzles to try to sort out, more agony to ponder.

I love You. Help me to love You more. Help the Durkins in this painful, poignant time of their lives.

April 9, 1994 — Chicago

My Love,

Yesterday was terrible. All week was terrible. The weekend is off, but my stomach is upset and I don't feel very well. Jack went home from the hospital yesterday and is back today with high heart beat and reduced blood pressure. I don't know how they stand it.

I'm a shambles, really am. Several people say how old and tired I look. Well, I should feel that way because I am old and dreadfully tired.

Sorry I missed this reflection yesterday. How can it be that always on Friday, the day I have class, there's something in the afternoon.

There was lots of positive affirmation at the meeting — an award and six very supportive papers. Too bad the papers don't have any effect on the Greeley myth. If I were not so beaten down right now, however, they would have been a real shot in the arm.

Only another month till the world slows down again. Help me to get through it.

April 10, 1994 — Chicago

My Love,

It will be nice to get back to writing stories, to being a story teller again. After some of the recent problems with publishers and agents I have been terribly discouraged about the stories.

As I remarked at the panel the other day I am one of the few authors who must actually fight with people not about plot or character or atmosphere or vision, but about what the stories are. Sometimes I think I'm losing that fight.

Yet the people at the popular culture meeting understand and so do hundreds of thousands of readers. I let myself grow discouraged too easily. And now, tired as I am, it is hard to bounce back from the discouragement. But this summer I hope to.

I'm going through the motions now, but at least I think I'm gathering materials to focus with. Help me in the busy four weeks that lie ahead.

I love You.

April 11, 1994 — Chicago

My Love,

Mary Jule is talking funeral now — an evening Mass and a party afterward, what Jack would want. Brave. But so much strain for so long a period of time. Take care of her and protect her and all the family.

I'll be back tomorrow with, I hope, more reflective prayer.

And, by the way, I hope they can fix my computer.

I love You.

April 12, 1994 — Chicago

My Love,

Rushing again. Off to a meeting about a possible TV series, then a stop at the Durkins. With any luck my computer will be fixed and I'll be able to get back to using it tomorrow and do the analysis for the book survey and dig out the Coleman talk tomorrow.

The poem I read the other day noted the oddity that Your son could walk on water in his own time and cannot walk in a poem today. That's not true in the sense that most Americans would be offended by a poem about Jesus but it is true that such a poem would not be published in a leading poetry journal no matter how good it was. Moreover, the face of Jesus has been so obscured by scholarly and religious quarrels and dogmas that it is perhaps more difficult to write poems about him because the minds of the (good) poets are confused about who He is and what He stands for.

The Gospels, properly read, are clear enough. But they are not often properly read. He was someone who came to tell us about Your love and to assure us that when we die we die with You. It's that simple, but somehow the utter simplicity of that message gets lost.

In the Church one hears much about sex, nothing about Your love. What the hell has gone wrong!

Anyway, I love You. Help me through this day and the days and weeks ahead.

April 13, 1994 — Chicago

My Love,

I stopped by the Durkins yesterday. Jack is much worse. Getting ready to go on a journey, he says. I can only say to

You now, please take him home and spare both him and his family any more suffering.

I love You.

April 16, 1994 — Chicago

My Love,

Jack died the day before yesterday. I've been running every second since then, no time to mourn, no time for anything. This weekend had been one of the most rigidly scheduled of my life. I've cancelled almost everything, but even to do that requires rushing. I'm empty, drained, and so, so tired. Maybe I can sort this all out eventually, but right now I can say only that I love You and I'll be back later.

April 17, 1994 — Chicago

My Love,

The funeral Mass is tonight, a wake before, a party after. Help me and all of them to hold up.

I need to mourn. I wonder if I will. My body mourns, even if I don't.

April 18, 1994 — Chicago

My Love,

"The most beautiful service," Sue Neal said, tears in her eyes, "I've ever been to." Norman and Carol Nie, their faces wet, couldn't say anything. Many said that it was the most beautiful funeral they had ever seen. All true, a tremendous tribute to Jack and the family. Mary Jule's eulogy was sensational; so was Dan's poem. Deeply, deeply moving.

The party afterward, as I told Miss Molly, was Irish Catholicism at its best. It was all of that.

And through it all I was dry and cold. Mind you my voice cracked a couple of times, so I was mourning like the rest. But I'm so tired and so numb that I can't reach the emotions that are inside me.

Often when the liturgy celebrated human survival, I found myself not believing a word of it.

Of course I believe it all, as You well know. But my weariness and exhaustion have dulled everything within me. I go through the motions and I guess go through them pretty well. But I need a couple of good night's sleep before I can pull together the emotions of this tragic time and integrate them into myself. Help me to do that.

Jack was an impressive man, his career cut short by bad health and the viciousness of the corporate world. But nothing could affect his worth and value and dignity as a human being, as the tribute last night showed.

Yet I feel hollow and empty and not merely because of the tragedy of loss and pain and separation. Things ought to have been better.

I love You. Help me please.

April 19, 1994 — Over Lake Michigan

My Love,

I didn't use to like cemeteries, perhaps because of the odd and, as I thought then, superstitious behavior of my aunts. I have visited my father's grave only once since 1947 and that to bury my mother in 1964. But yesterday, understanding better the symbolism and the metaphor of burial, I found the cemetery an oddly reassuring and peaceful place. After Jack was buried I sought out the graves of my parents — which is where I will be buried when it is Your pleasure to call me home — and also found some kind of peace and reassurance. It is only part of them, part of Jack, and eventually part of me that will lie in the ground at Queen of Heaven cemetery. The rest of us will be elsewhere, awaiting or in some sense already participating in the resurrection of the dead and the life of the world to come.

Mary Jule was wonderful, as she has been through all these days. After the service, while we were standing around talking, the young undertaker discretely waited for us to leave before lowering the casket into the ground. She turned and said, "That's all right, Patrick, you can lower it now, it won't bother us," and returned to the conversation.

Very impressive indeed.

The peace I discovered out there on Wolf Road was that there is nothing unusual about my reactions or non-reactions. (I almost broke down at the service. Too bad, perhaps, that I didn't.) They are a combination of tragedy and pre-existing exhaustion. I was already worn from the strenuous demands of these busy weeks and Jack's death was a kick in the gut that exhausted me all the more. Death does not fit anyone's schedule, does it? My own won't either. Looking back on the last year, I must ask myself whether there was any time I could have coped better.

I think there was. Last week and this week are the busiest of the year — hence my trip to Washington today and tomorrow.

Anyway I love You and I thank You for the gift of faith and of a little peace. Now if I can only have a solid night of sleep I'll be a lot better.

April 20, 1994 — Washington, D.C.

My Love,

I have finally "caught up" on sleep for which many, many thanks. I now have the resources to reflect on Jack's death. First of all, my jumbled feelings last week were the result of weariness and should not be a cause for concern. Secondly, he was a good and great man and it is most unfortunate that we were not closer. As Mike Hout said in his E-mail message yesterday, he was a naturally and genuinely funny man whose laughter was always both contagious and gentle. As for not being closer, surely it was in part my doing, though finally I could have done little about it, given the source of the problem. That was tragic, but a lot of life's tragedies are inevitable.

Moreover, as the plot of land out there at the cemetery makes clear, soon I will be laid to rest too. A lot of my compulsive work makes no difference at all and will make no difference when that happens. While an occasional week like these last couple may be necessary, I don't have to live that way; I shouldn't live that way; I especially shouldn't let myself be separated from Your love by the need to rush, rush, rush. That means cutting back, which I surely propose to do.

Finally (for the moment) the faith and hope and love of the family and its deep impression on everyone that was at the funeral are an epiphany about what Catholicism means and one at which I should rejoice. I thank You for our tradition and I love You.

April 21, 1994 — Chicago

My Love,

Jack's death makes me think that I ought to prepare for my own. I reflect also on what my death will be like compared to his. There will be no family to rally round, no one to hover at the death bed, no one to arrange any of the details that need arranging. Therefore I must make all the plans beforehand so that no one will be burdened or forced to do what they don't want to do.

None of the above matters all that much because, regardless, I'll still be dead.

And alive.

I must die, however, as I have lived — a man of faith and hope. Teilhard used to write to his friends how important it was that he made a "good death." Important for others that he give example. Important for himself that he be loyal to You to the end.

He finally died alone, as did Your son. If that be the way it is for me, I accept that. Help me to accept.

I don't think I'm morbid about these things. I just want to think them through and be ready. I believe that Jack lives and that we all shall live with You — though I have no idea of what that means.

I am not eager to celebrate my anniversary on Sunday, not with all the lingering grief/joy of this past weekend — and in the same venue at that. My heart won't be in it and neither, alas, will be my stomach.

But celebrate we must, so celebrate I will. Maybe, in a Durkheim mode, the external celebration will get to me internally. I hope it does because I have so much to be grateful for in my forty years in the priesthood.

April 24, 1994 — Chicago

My Love,

Well, today is the celebration of forty years in the priesthood and I could not feel less celebratory. Most of my reactions are damn foolishness, and I would not be having

them if a mixture of grief and weariness were not domi-
nating my life just now. I'll do my best this afternoon and
evening and with Your help I will carry it off. That's all I
can expect.

In my head I realize that the last four decades have been
graceful and grace-filled years. I am surely one of that 57
percent who say that the priesthood is better than I had
expected and the 70 percent who say they would certainly
do it again. I am deeply grateful to You for my vocation,
more grateful than I have ever been and for all the special graces that came my way during the last forty years. I
am sorry for all my mistakes and I am thankful that You
have prevented them from being worse. I am also sorry for
my failure to use my talents always as I should and for so
often working myself into a state of exhaustion.

I am grateful especially for the excitement and the fun
and the challenge of the last forty years. They have been
truly extraordinary, and they seem likely to continue, at
least for a little while.

I am grateful for my friends, priests and lay, and for my
family and for all those who have stood by me through the
years in good times and bad. I am grateful for the health
and energy that have generally remained with me. I am
thankful for the wit that has stood me in such good stead
at the hard times.

I am dazzled, as I finish the reflection, at how good
You've been to me. I don't deserve it, but I am very
happy for Your generosity. Help me in return to be generous to others and begin this afternoon by generosity in
celebration.

I love You. That's the biggest gift of all of the last
forty years — coming to know You a little better and to
understand Your love a little more.

April 25, 1994 — Chicago

My Love,

Yesterday was grand, brilliant, as the Irish would say. A real shot in the arm, even if I was exhausted. Jack Shea had some good things to say about my role as someone who challenges others, individuals and institutions, to be more fully themselves. That is surely what I do, though I had never quite thought of it that way before. The people around seemed to agree. If that be what I do, it is an activity that carries with it considerable risk. Mind you, I don't intend to stop.

For a while yesterday I really felt that my forty years as a priest had not been wasted. That's a strange thing to say, isn't it? I know they haven't been wasted, but there's a difference between knowing it and *feeling* it. It strikes me that for a long time I have haven't felt that — because of the constant attacks and the people who once liked me and don't seem to any more. The battering catches up, especially when, while one knows the charges aren't true, the allies are silent.

It's the *feeling*, I mean, and one of the results of the *feeling* might be this weariness.

Anyway thanks for the good time last night and for the good forty years.

April 28, 1994 — Chicago

My Love,

Bluebells and daffodils and flowering trees and bushes! The arboretum was gorgeous even if it turned cold and gray at the end of the day (and is winter again today!). It was early, very early spring yesterday, that first fragile venture of spring in which it seems not altogether confident that it will survive or that it wants to stay. Not full-blown spring but the early adolescence of spring.

How beautiful You must be to generate such beauty as a reflection of Yourself. And on just one small planet in an immense cosmos. Do they have spring in other places? Do they have bluebells and daffodils? Or do they have even more appealing sacraments? I wonder! In both senses.

It was so peaceful out there. Three hours of wandering in natural beauty — with an expressway only a couple of hundred yards away! Still it was lovely and quiet and filled with acres of daffodils and honking geese. So it wasn't quiet. Nature is never quiet. But it was a different kind of noise. I found myself asking, wouldn't that be a better life than listening for the phone and rushing for E-mail.

Probably not, in truth. At least not for me. But I need more interludes like that, especially in these times of frantic rush.

I had intended today to be a quiet day. Obviously now it won't be. I'll be off to Europe in a rush. Grant that when I come back I can reassert control over my life.

And help me to remember for the next few days the bluebells and the daffodils.

April 29, 1994 — Chicago

My Love,

I'm at O'Hare waiting for boarding for the trip to Milano. Another horrific day. Class, an emergency trip to the dentist to have my splint glued back in, a book left in the car on the way out, and a guy here in the Ambassador Club who wanted to pick a fight because I was using his telephone. He tried to pull the wire out of the phone. I simply walked away from him, though the temptation to fight back was pretty strong.

I was wearing my priest suit too. The guy must be a real jerk because his wife walked away when he began to insult me. Poor woman.

Anyway, I'm off on this crazy trip, about which I ought to have known better I suppose — four cities and four hotels in eleven days, four plane flights and two train rides, so I'll be on the move five of those eleven days.

It will be exciting if I don't poop out somewhere along the line — like tomorrow!

No matter how exhausting this trip, it cannot be any worse than the last six weeks. I hope things are not so bad when I come back.

Please take care of me on this trip. I love You.

April 30, 1994 — Milano

My Love,

The chaos of my life continues to catch up with me. I lost my passport twice (found it both times, for that many thanks) and have discovered that I came without (a) an electric shaver (b) disks for this machine, (c) the modem which would have enabled me to use CompuServe (d) the parallel interface cable for my printer. So I have all the equipment for E-mail and printing except the essentials. These oversights are about as strong a judgment on my lifestyle as one can imagine. Yet I don't see how I can avoid these mistakes unless I have packets prepared for overseas travel long before the travel begins — including a shaver. I'll have to see to that when I get back.

I'm stumbling and bumbling around and I definitely need protection by Your angels or You Yourself if You have the time.

At least this machine is working, but all the attachments that were supposed to make me a sophisticated traveler are back in Chicago.

The good news is that lunch with Cardinal Martini went very well. He is a very impressive man and would indeed make an excellent Pope. Moreover, he has read my work and understands it, which of course makes him even more impressive to me. Finally, he laughed at my jokes through lunch, which was most impressive of all!

I'm tired so I'm going to try to sleep regardless of what time it is in Chicago.

I love You. Please keep an eye on me.

May 1994

May 7, 1994 — Rome

My Love,

A late entry tonight because of the wedding this morning and a ride over to Mike Hout's hotel to arrange for our trip to Tel Aviv tomorrow. Only three more nights before I'm home.

There was wall-to-wall people over at the Piazza de Spagna. Saturday night in Rome — what a vital city it is! In a way the world's first city in terms of age and cultural influence out of the past. I'm not so sure, however, that it is a good thing for our Catholic heritage to be so closely identified with it. But then what are the alternatives? If one wants to see the Catholic heritage and the Catholic imagination at its best and its worst, this is the place to do it. Maybe the worst is necessary so that one can have the best. It's been a long time, more than a decade, since I've been here. Things have changed a lot with more rapid transit and a lot more respect for pedestrians. Tomorrow I'll recall my experiences yesterday afternoon when I drifted into San Pietro and the memories came flooding back. However, tonight I want to reflect on the wedding today. It was a warm and romantic and very happy event, and I am glad I was able to fit it into my schedule. They are good young people as were all the rather small crowd that was here. And a wedding in St. Peter's is a classy idea.

One terrible blight on it, however: just as I was starting the Eucharistic Prayer, the *parocho*, the parish priest, came rushing up to the altar and shook his finger warningly about Chris's bare shoulders (chaste shoulders on a chaste young women). She had to be veiled with a mantle before the ceremonies went on, much to the disgust of the civilized Irish Catholics who were at the ceremony.

Later he explained to the Paulist priest who had made the arrangements that he was sorry and that he would not have done it but Cardinal Noe's secretary (a prim and mean-looking fellow) had shown up and he would have been reported if he didn't intervene. Well, it's nice that we're doing what we ought to do, isn't it? One member of the wedding party was banned from San Pietro yesterday because her hemline was not below the knee. Nothing changes. As Brian Burns remarked at the dinner, it's astonishing that they get away with what they get away with. Mostly they do, I think, because of our loyalty. But it is all going to have to stop or the loyalty will fade away — as it has already on many matters that these folks around here think are important.

We should be and could be so much better.

Anyway I love You, and I thank You for the graces and the memories, both good and bad, of these last two days in Rome. Now on to the last phase of what has certainly been an exciting trip. I love You.

May 9, 1994 — Tel Aviv

My Love,

I'm not sure where Tel Aviv is in relationship to Galilee, probably part of it but there's no evidence in the Scripture that Your son ever ventured over in this direction. It certainly has changed since his time. Sitting here on the balcony of the hotel, looking out over the sun-drenched white buildings and pools and the sea, I might be in Los Angeles or Florida or maybe Bahia. The ISSP meeting goes well, though the subject matter for this year has not been conceptualized as well as it might have been. All in all it's very exciting, and I thank You for giving me the opportunity to become involved. I'm actually looking forward to greater involvement with the Germans at the Zentral Archiv and with the Italians and of course with the Irish.

I was especially interested in a report from the Russians that confirms my own work. You're having a field day there just now, which is astonishing to almost everyone.

One more day of meetings and then a departure for the twenty-hour trip to Chicago. I've done that before from here, though it was twenty-five years ago. I'm not looking forward to it. But I wish to thank You for an interesting and exciting trip.

I love You. Take care of me please on the trip home.

May 21, 1994 — Chicago

My Love,

Nine hours sleep last night and a half hour swim this morning and the world looks good. Bulls won last night too, another triumph over the powers of darkness. I'm off to Grand Beach this evening. The terrible two months after my return from Tucson are over.

I saw Mary Jule last night. A woman of great and powerful faith, as are all the kids.

I hope at the lake to get everything back on track, including my spiritual reading, which I desperately need.

I love You.

May 23, 1994 — Grand Beach, Michigan

My Love,

I'm reading Yeats, a book that has been at my spiritual reading post since last summer. He sure is lyrical! Now he is lamenting the fact that he and his love are growing old and their beauty is fading. Something worth lamenting. Growing old is filled with sorrow. Yet the research of Thorstam I read last week is fascinating in its suggestions about wisdom. There is, it would seem, a propensity to grow detached as one grows older, but it is a detachment that points toward the transcendent, a detachment that leads to more attachment. Like facing the end and seeing it's not all that bad.

I love You. Help me to love You more. Help me to realize that in the implacability of Your love nothing ever really fades.

May 29, 1994 — Grand Beach, Michigan

My Love,

What two incredibly beautiful days, almost unbearably beautiful. The beginning of summer is the best of all times because summer in its entirety stretches out with its never-ending (as we would like it) promises. This is the most beautiful Memorial Day weekend in the almost thirty years I've had this house.

Perfect summer in miniature — Mass on the lawn, kids on the beach, teenagers on golf carts, older couples walking, often hand in hand, the stuff of poetry if I can get in a poetry mood.

This summer I must enjoy it more than ever to show my gratitude to You.

Thank You for the magic.

May 30, 1994 — Grand Beach, Michigan

My Love,

Another glorious day, three in a row. For which many, many thanks.

I continue in my blessed lethargy, struggling to emerge from it, which perhaps I shouldn't do.

I continue to love summer and to believe that it is a most powerful sacrament of Your goodness and beauty.

I love You.

June 1994

June 2, 1994 — Grand Beach, Michigan

My Love,

I finished the book on the Iraq war yesterday and put aside the D-Day book because I decided I did not want to read it. The former was horrific enough. Enormous American fire power not only slaughtered tens of thousands of Iraqis, it also slaughtered many of our own through "friendly" (what a joke!) fire. You give nervous kids that kind of weaponry and they are surely going to shoot at everything in sight. Then you don't finish what you started. The Panama invasion writ large. I was right to oppose it then and am still right, even though it was a "great victory."

War shows humankind at its worst. And yet it still goes on all over the world. A good question is why You permit it. And a good answer is that You probably can't stop it — not once You had created free beings with what passes for reason.

Yet in the face of it all I affirm that I believe in Your love and assert my love for You in return.

June 6, 1994 — Grand Beach, Michigan

My Love,

D-Day plus fifty. For some odd reason the media have gone wild on the commemoration of the Normandy landing. It surely was a historic event and perhaps the outstanding accomplishment of the war, but it seems like overkill to me.

The day ought to be remembered, but things like beach landings at Montrose harbor are weird. Most of those who are enthusing about the landing in the papers and on TV were either not alive or not comprehending in those days. They don't have the context and they don't really understand. A jerk writing in the *Washington Post* dismissed it as a slaughter of innocents. Apparently he was so ignorant of history that he didn't realize that the slaughter was really taking place in the concentration camps and that it was to put an end to Hitler and what the camps stood for that the landing occurred.

Studs Terkel wrote a book a number of years ago about "the good war," an ironic title suggesting that it wasn't good at all. All wars are bad, and WWII was no exception. But sometimes there is no choice but to fight. That was one of those times.

The deeper problem is the mystery of evil that put madmen in power in Germany, Russia, and Japan, men who were responsible for at least a hundred million deaths and maybe almost twice as many. Someone said that it was a war between a lie and a half truth. Maybe, but a bit of truth is better than no truth at all.

War continues to be a mystery to me. I know You don't want it, but it happens just the same with all its slaughter and cruelty. Maybe at last we're leaving that behind, but then there's Bosnia and Rwanda.

So that leaves me in mystery, much more against war

than I was in 1944, nostalgic for the memories of those times, and baffled by humankind.

It's not a mystery I'll ever solve. I end up as I always do with the notion that You loved every single one of those people who died not only on D-Day but through the whole war and that You will wipe every tear away from their eyes.

And so I love You too.

June 11, 1994 — Grand Beach, Michigan

My Love,

The various passages in the Gospel I read this morning deal with obeying the law in our heart. What Your son demands of us is not legalism but love. This can be in theory a dangerous position because it permits people who claim they are acting out of love ("no one is hurt!") to flout all norms and rules. But the opposite position, a cold, hard, literalistic legalism of the sort that some fundamentalists practice (including Catholic fundamentalists) is one in which religion is reduced to parsing sacred texts. Jesus knew that kind of religion and condemned it. The law must be permeated by love to be religious. That means the individual decisions must be made, agonizing individual decisions, and that there is no substitute for that agony. The Church ought to try to provide its people with skills in making such decisions instead of trying to take away their freedom and force them all to do exactly what the letter of the law demands.

Ending a marriage, for example. Sometimes one should. Sometimes one shouldn't. It was perhaps too hard once, and now it is perhaps too easy. But what do individuals do? What should they do? Tough decision. Same thing about leaving the priesthood.

I think I am reasonably free of the old legalism (I can think of some times when I tried to enforce the law without love and I regret them very much), and I'm also free, I hope, from the self-pitying anarchism of the sixties.

For this tenuous balance I am grateful to You for guidance, and I am aware that I could relax into the easy feeling that I have it all figured out, another form of legalism replacing love.

I will finish the novel today and begin to relax for a couple of days before my trip to Germany. And I've got my Aero computer functioning again, at least pretty well. But it's been a tough week.

June 12, 1994 — Grand Beach, Michigan

My Love,

The word from Your son this morning is to beware of the scribes and Pharisees. I couldn't help but reflect on the enormous risks the archdiocese is taking of looking like scribes and Pharisees in this North Brook case in which they could lose seven million dollars. The word I have is that the ruthless cross-examinations of the boy and his grandmothers by the Church's lawyers did not play well with the jury.

I wonder if all the Church can do is play such hardball. I still am not sure about what really happened up there, but I know what's happening in court, and it doesn't look good for us.

I can understand why the Cardinal didn't listen to me and settle the case, but I fear for what's going to happen.

We make it so difficult for ourselves, don't we? I hope and pray that this ends well and that especially justice is done.

I love You.

June 13, 1994 — Grand Beach, Michigan

My Love,

The novel is finished — 108,000 words, 28,000 more than I had anticipated (but still within the upper limitations). It was fun to write, the most fun yet and probably the best yet. I hope someone likes it. I was utterly exhausted yesterday when I finished running the spelling programs. It's also hard work. But that's all right.

The readings from the Scripture today emphasize fidelity in the heart. I am impressed again by Your son's distaste for hypocrisy, especially since most Christian leaders have little awareness of their own constant hypocrisy. I think He'd be as upset with us as He was with the scribes and Pharisees. More so perhaps because it is all done in Your name. Not just us, all denominations, but perhaps worse among us because we claim so much in His name.

It is sickening, disgusting, horrible. It probably can't be stopped, but certainly we could cut some of it if we were not so arrogant, not so close-minded, not so proud. Despite the Second Vatican Council we haven't changed all that much, from Rome on down.

There's not much I can do except write about hypocrisy in my stories and articles.

Help us to reform, really reform,

I love You.

June 20, 1994 — Cologne

My Love,

I'm afraid I ate too much chocolate ice cream the last couple of days.

I also hope that in my advanced state of tiredness I did

a good job here. I think I did, but I can never be sure in a foreign culture. I think I puzzle them as both a priest and a sociologist, but that's all right too.

Eckhart and I were eating ice cream in Arweiler the day before yesterday and I made a goofy comment about chocolate ice cream reflecting You. He said, half in fun and half in earnest, that more and more he liked this God of mine.

But that God is really You, isn't it? Ice cream, especially chocolate ice cream, is a sacrament of Your sweetness. How did things ever get so badly confused that people do not realize that? If we had not so obscured Your image there would be a lot less religious decline in Europe. But we — and especially the fools in the Vatican — have equated You with sexual repression. No wonder people don't think of You as the God of chocolate ice cream. But You are just the same.

And for that and for all the other good things that You also are, I love You.

June 22, 1994 — Bonn-Cologne Airport

My Love,

How often in my life have I sat in an airport at this hour of the morning, sleepy, thirsty, worn. It goes with the territory, I guess.

A good long weekend here. It's nice occasionally to be the expert, indeed the revered expert from out of town. Also the Rhenish hospitality has been outstanding.

I met Michele and Rick yesterday and spent the afternoon and early evening with them. We did the renewal of vows in the sacrament chapel of the Cologne Cathedral. Seven years and they're still very happy, in part because they complement each other so nicely.

We talked about the bombing that wiped out 90 percent of Cologne fifty years ago. The Brits didn't bomb factories; they bombed cities and didn't care how many people they killed. We at least went after factories, though perhaps only one out of ten bombs fell in the target area. A lot of civilian deaths, hundreds of thousands at least. The Germans started the raids on civilian populations, but that hardly justified what we did to them.

No doubt the war was necessary. How else could Hitler have been stopped. Yet it was a terrible thing, a lot more terrible than I could or did realize when I was a teen, so long ago and yet only yesterday. The Germans who are a little younger, my colleagues, seem to accept what happened with little anger. Rather they look at the economic and political "miracle" and to the future, though they worry about the resurgent Nazis here and Fascists in Italy. If I were they, I'd worry too.

Humankind can be and still is both brutal and stupid.

It will be good to get home.

Thank You for the trip.

I love You.

June 26, 1994 — Grand Beach, Michigan

My Love,

I've been reading the Frank Tripler book in which You are depicted as the computer at the center of everything gathering together all the light waves of the universe and thus giving meaning and love and eternal life to everyone. Fascinating scheme. Theology, he says, is a branch of physics. You and all You stand for can be proven by physics.

I think he goes a little far, but it certainly fits some of what I believe. I incline to think that we can prove with a high degree of probability Your existence and Your nature. But that does not mean there is no need for faith too.

A computer indeed but a loving computer, unlike the ones I'm still struggling with this morning.

You know how hard it is to work with my present keyboard problems. So You'll understand why I'm stopping now. I love You, computer or not.

July 1994

July 5, 1994 — Grand Beach, Michigan

My Love,

I'm reading American poets for my spiritual reading, now John Crowe Ransom, who this morning laments the failing of womanly beauty. One merely has to walk the beach as I did yesterday to realize the sad truth of this observation. Ditto I might add for manly beauty, which is less beautiful even at its best (at least as a man perceives it and perhaps as an angel would perceive it too). My research on the perception of womanly beauty reveals that this deterioration does not happen in the eyes of the beloved. Simple observation also demonstrates that there are women in their sixties who are beautiful by any objective standard also. Yet beauty does deteriorate in some fashion and often early in life and often because of emotional problems because of which a woman wants not to appear beautiful.

For the poet this is a sign of the fragility of human life. How right he is! How fragile we are. So lovely in our beginnings and so ugly and tragic in our deterioration and our endings. I continue to hang on to life, to cling to it though I know it is fragile and that my days are numbered and that all human events eventually end badly.

Not a very hopeful thought for the beginning of summer is it?

Especially not when I realize that, having begun, summer has also begun to end.

What remains?

You and Your promise that all will be well and all will be well and all manner of things will be well.

And we will all be beautiful again.

I believe in Your love. In a sense that is all I have. My main spiritual challenge should be to believe more deeply and more powerfully in that love. I hope to work on it this summer in the face of all the difficulty and tragedy that lurks around me.

The young women on the beach who are so attractive will lose their beauty, one way or another, but they will become beautiful again because You love them and You delight in their beauty and You delight in all of us.

And therein is our grounds for our hope and our life.

July 6, 1994 — Grand Beach, Michigan

My Love,

I continue to reflect on John Crowe Ransom's poem (and what a perfect southern name he has!) about women. The other night as we were eating supper on the deck down at the beach, a cruiser that had been anchored near the shore was preparing to depart as haze and sunset turned the lake into a shadowy wonderland. A woman in the water clung to the rail of the boat and bounced up and down, rocking the boat and pulling herself off the lake bottom in a display of playful exuberance. In the encroaching darkness she was a silhouette, a graceful line drawn against the gray and silver lake. She was a tall, slender line, extending herself tautly to her full height as she tugged against the boat, curved only at her breasts, a special grace in the shadows.

It was a brief silent image, erotic as all graceful women are, but more revelatory than erotic, a hint of Grace, of Exuberance, of Mystery, and of Love, a special sight on a beach that in the course of the weekend offered many lovely attractions, especially because of the sharpness of her form and the briefness of her presence before night arrived and she and her boat disappeared.

Ransom is wrong that her beauty, caught in that transient moment, will fade forever. It will fade, but the moment of grace will not fade and eventually her youthful exuberance (though how youthful she was I do not know) will return and persist. That I know and believe.

You would not, could not create such grace and then let it perish forever.

And therefore I love You, giver of life and beauty and hope.

July 7, 1994 — Grand Beach, Michigan

My Love,

It is the Great Depression child in me that was rocked yesterday by the failure to obtain a contract for *Angel Light*. My career as a story teller is in shambles and may never escape from the low ebb it has reached.

I'm better today than I was yesterday. Indeed my resilience surprises me. I can't say this failure is unimportant because it's not. But I can say that it is not all-important. I've been through bad times before and have bounced back. If You be willing, I will do so this time too.

In a way I'm not surprised. I kind of knew that this would happen.

I thought the reason would be that people don't like

my novels. That wasn't true. They still like them and the stories are better than ever. The problems are part of the nuttiness of the business, and I didn't expect that.

Anyway I trust in Your love and that everything will work out one way or another. I will not go into a midsummer depression.

I love You. Sustain my hope and cheer through this difficult time.

July 8, 1994 — Grand Beach, Michigan

My Love,

I didn't sleep too well last night — only four hours — and have been bumbling and stumbling around this morning. I suppose the failure of the auction of *Angel Light* was still bugging my unconscious, even though I am more or less adjusted consciously. It always takes time for the depths of the personality to catch up. To be candid (that I had always better be with You), it is the sense of failure which probably bugs me. In truth I did not and have not failed. On the contrary I have had an extraordinary run of success as a novelist and a tremendous impact. The success may be over (or it may not be over) but that doesn't mean that I have failed. If it were published, who knows how many copies it would sell and how many people it would touch?

Still it hurts, as rejection always does.

Which You know very well, having been rejected so often Yourself.

I must go on confidently and cheerfully to whatever is the next challenge in life.

Which does not mean that the fiction career is over. However, I must be prepared for the possibility that it is greatly diminished. It looked like forever, as the Mark

Harris novel says in its title. Fifteen years is not a bad run and for that I'm grateful and I love You.

I must keep saying these things to myself over and over again, and maybe I'll begin to persuade my unconscious!

I must snap out of the dumps, with Your help.

And I am grateful for the wondrous surprise of my career as a novelist. I anticipate more surprises in life because You are a God of wonder and surprise.

July 14, 1994 — Grand Beach, Michigan

My Love,

More Conrad Aiken poetry this morning — the anguished cry of an old man who wants to die because he has lost so much of himself and those he loved. Most of his poems in the collection I am reading echo the same theme. I am in no position to judge him (or anyone else). I am growing old, but I am not yet ready to beg to die, much less to consider self-destruction. Yet I can see how life could lose its savor. Even now I wonder whether my magic is gone, my time spent, my talents exhausted — a foolish notion given my piece in the *Times* on Sunday. Yet that piece took on perhaps too much importance for me precisely because it proves that I still have the magic.

What happens when I lose it?

Hopefully I'll still do my best with what I have and keep trying.

I read Boris Yeltsin's book last night, an impressively humble and human person. How fragile it is what he's trying to do and how honest he is about his own mistakes. Protect him in his efforts; so much of peace for the world still depends on Russia.

And comparing my tasks with his, how easy I have it.

This looks like it's going to be another one of those bad days. At noon I go to the beach regardless.

I love You.

July 18, 1994 — Grand Beach, Michigan

My Love,

Back to Chicago again this morning to see the dentist. Like I say, Irish teeth!

Take care of me on this trip. Help me to realize how fragile I am, how dependent on Your love and grace and how puny and unimportant my plans and hopes are on a day when comet fragments crash into Jupiter and produce the "biggest blast in the history of the solar system." A blast that is tiny compared to all the blasts You have going on in the comsos all the time — to say nothing of the Biggest Bang of all.

Of what sort are You *really*, a God of love but wild violent love? No point in trying to figure You out. No love can ever be figured out.

But I do love You.

July 26, 1994 — Grand Beach, Michigan

My Love,

I began reading today Henri Nouwen's new book, *Here and Now*. He talks about prayer as the hub of life. To pray is to move to the center of life and of love. How true. We spend so much time in the distractions of the spokes that we lose our centering in the hub of prayer. In a lifetime of praying and of serious attempts to pray, I have never quite made it into the hub in such a way as to center myself. The distractions dominate my life. I live in the here and now, which is where we all live, but I am dominated by the here and now. Sadness over this domination and my inability to sustain contact with You and Your love in the here and now permeates my life. I feel at times like I have wasted my life on distractions and permitted things like mail and phone and guests and demands interfere not only with the best of my work but also with the whole purpose of life.

Like this morning, I have so many things to do when I wake up that the day seems like a waste even before I begin. What folly!

Help me to love You more and to pray better so that I will find the center of my life while I still have time. Tomorrow I will start writing my psalms in Your praise.

I love You.

July 27, 1994 — Grand Beach, Michigan

My Love,

PSALM FOR A SUMMER DAY

I praise You in the ice-white jet
As it cuts softly across the sapphire sky
And trails whisps of fragile frozen mist
Dissolving into blue

In the stiff wings of sea birds
As they soar above the dunes
With loud cries of hope and love
Searching for their noonday meal

In the sand warm and soft
Slyly tugging at my toes
Like it did long ago
When I was a little boy

> I praise You in the determined lake
> Doggedly building up the beach
> I sing of You as You play in the surging waves
> White caps dissolving into foam

I really do see You in all those sights and sounds. Help me to see You everywhere.

I'll continue these psalms and then come back each day to do revisions.

I love You.

July 29, 1994 — Grand Beach, Michigan

My Love,

Book-of-the-Month bought *Irish Gold*, the first good news in the fiction world for the last year. Thank You very much!

I love You.

July 30, 1994 — Grand Beach, Michigan

My Love,

I must, as Nouwen said the other day, choose for joy. Today he says we must be surprised by joy, by the joyous look on a little kid's face when he finds a kitten in the yard. Or one of the kids I talked to last night as I was repairing the rearview mirror. That joy is about what is really real.

I love You.

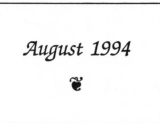

August 1994

August 4, 1994 — Grand Beach, Michigan

My Love,

I will try to begin my psalm for a rainy day today, which is surely a rainy day.

> I praise You in the ominous clouds
> Gray on black, charging across the lake
> In the nervous sea birds' shrill complaint
> As the water turns green and still
>
> I sing of You in the sudden wind
> That whips up instant white-fringed waves
> Slams the oak trees, bends the maples
> And rattles my roof and window panes
>
> I recognize You in the lightning
> As it carves the distant sky
> In the thunder clap just above my head
> And in the rain beating against the house
>
> I see You in the dripping trees
> And the reviving flower buds
> In the humid air as the storm moves on
> And the shining puddles on the street

I thank You in the grass renewed
And the singing robins
In the return of sunshine
And all the gifts of summer

Amen

August 5, 1994 — Grand Beach, Michigan

My Love,

More good news on books. *Irish Gold* is now a main selection of the Book-of-the-Month Club, and the new Blackie novel an alternate for the Mystery Club. All of a sudden the tide seems to be turning. I am as baffled by the good news as I have been by the bad for the last year and a half. But grateful for the seeming turn of the tide. Grant that the change persist. However, as I reflected a few days ago, I rejoice in the present and trust the future to You.

I love You.

August 17, 1994 — Grand Beach, Michigan

My Love,

Why are all the American poets I read so obsessed with death? Maybe because they are part of an elite culture that has given up on religion. Maybe because faith is not fashionable in the poetry culture. Maybe because religion has not responded adequately to the questions of men and women who are sensitive enough to be poets. But surely there is not a single expression of faith in the whole lot of them. To a person they reject the possibility of hope (with the exception, as I have noted before, of Red Warren). Pretty grim.

You sent Your son to confirm the human instinct that there are grounds for hope. If there are such grounds, then the whole ambience of our existence is transformed. Yet how the Church has obscured and corrupted that message or perverted it for institutional goals. The answer is not to walk away but to try to reform the institution and refresh the message. But the resistance to such change is enormous, as I well know, having banged my head up against it all my life as a priest and ended up on the margins of the Church for doing so.

I'm into the new Blackie now, and it's coming along fine. It fits what's on my mind because it is a parish story, and much can be said about You and faith in that context without twisting the story.

Help me to do it well. I love You.

August 19, 1994 — Grand Beach, Michigan

My Love,

I finished reading the new chapters Joe [Blotner] sent me in his biography of Red Warren. What a fascinating and gifted man!

I was fascinated by the reviews of his books Joe cites. Red was probably the greatest literary man in the history of the country. He won three Pulitzer prizes, two for poetry and one for fiction. Yet how eager were the reviewers to destroy him, to claim that he had lost his talents, that his work was not as good as it used to be, and that a given book was "not his best." (Why must any book be the best?). In retrospect the reviewers look like nasty, mean-spirited, envious people. If they had any sense they would have realized that at the time. But the power to drag down a great was too much for them to worry about what judgments would be made about *their* work.

At least in the book reviews I write I lean over backward to be fair and never engage in the vicious art of tearing down the mighty.

The point here, however, is that if Red, one of the greats, became an ink blot for the puny and the stupid, I cannot expect to escape similar treatment. I am not great, but I am successful, and that's enough for the mean-spirited, especially mean-spirited priests and ex-priests, to try to destroy me.

I accept that as part of the human condition, as something that goes with the territory. But it still makes me angry. I must learn to get over the anger quickly and not act out of it. The strongly positive mail I get should be enough.

As well as Your love and support.

I love You. Help me to love You more.

August 23, 1994 — Grand Beach, Michigan

My Love,

Your son said that the very hairs of our head are counted, that not a sparrow falls that You do not know about, and that we are far more loved than the lilies of the field. Such is the nature of His experience of You. Now that is impressive language, perhaps the most impressive and most powerful description of You that anyone has ever spoken.

In the teeth of all the evil and suffering in the world, Jesus asserts the tender compassion of Your love, a tenderness and a compassion that are almost unbelievable. I have a hard time reconciling the God of the Big Bang and the God of fire and explosion on the one hand and this tender, loving God on the other. The chaos and destruction in the cosmos and gentle care seem so opposed to one another.

But as You would doubtless insist in reply, who do I think I am that I can figure You out? You are beyond my computational abilities and because I cannot harmonize the various aspects of You proves only that I am limited and You are not.

But I must keep the hairs of the head image in my mind, oh, me of little faith, as Jesus said in this context.

You do love and care for us all like a gentle and passionate parent, and that I do believe. Therefore I entrust myself and those I love to You (especially this morning Marilyn and Shags, both of whom are ill) with confidence that all manner of things will be well.

I love You.

August 25, 1994 — Grand Beach, Michigan

My Love,

Up in the early hours again, the result of a frantic battle with the mail last night. I now dread the mail with all its demands. It is the greatest single nuisance in my life. I worry about Marilyn too, though her fever seems to be gone. Please take care of her.

I had a long letter from a sociological colleague (not Catholic) who knows me only through my books. She has read the two prayer diaries and chides me gently for not appreciating the reactions of those who like my work and the influence it has. No doubt she's right (I wrote her and told her she should be my spiritual director!). Yet these are, as You know, dry times in my life. I seem to be fighting on all fronts and losing on most of them.

That's a silly thing to say, isn't it? I'm sorry. I'm so tired just now. I'll feel better in the morning.

Objectively she's right. I have accomplished an incredible amount of stuff. Yet the more I do the more hatred I stir up, which I guess is par for the course. There are times when it is just too much. Yet You have sent love into my life too, all kinds of it. I continue to be surprised by it and yet I also let the hatred outweigh the love, which is dumb.

Yet I do often feel dry these days and sad. It's not just the end of summer. Maybe it's aging, maybe it's the pace of life. I must do something to restore some of the missing joy that has somehow slipped away.

Like a day of recollection as soon as possible.

I'm going to try to get back to sleep now. Help me to love You more. Please take care of Marilyn.

August 26, 1994 — Grand Beach, Michigan

My Love,
    Marilyn is fine. Thank You very much.
    Guests, so I'm running.
    But I love You.

August 29, 1994 — Grand Beach, Michigan

My Love,
    The Irish Waterways IV series ended last night with a quote from a Quaker poet that I didn't get exactly but it went something like this: "The Universe is singing and we should listen carefully to it so we can join the chorus."

It's singing today with the wind straining the flags and the waves pounding the beach. I listen to the song, I hear it, I enjoy it, but I'm thinking of the calls I have to make, the mail I have to send, the errands I have to run, the dentists I have to visit, the crises (two or three anyway) I have to cope with. I've missed really hearing the singing all summer, maybe all my life. I see no hope that I'll ever be able to really hear it, much less join. Certainly not in the autumn that lies ahead of me.

I'm sorry. I know it's not right. I know I do too much. I know that I am compulsive about responsibilities. Take the upcoming Irish trip. It's limited to eight days because I have sermons here at both beginning and end. Foolish. Except how could I have said no to either situation. Would You want me to say no? I doubt it.

I need to figure some things out. How often have I said that in the past. But if I ever want to join the singing, I'm going to have to make some changes.

August 30, 1994 — Grand Beach, Michigan

My Love,

I read Red Warren's poem about hope and the classic line about how the moon bathes the world in white forgiveness when the last vestige of light seems to be gone. Talk about a sacramental imagination!

I should be singing with the moon, if the moon comes up these days, which I haven't noticed.

Remember all the poems I wrote about the moon, about You of course, since the moon represents You. But the poems are forgotten and I don't see the moon and I stumble on blindly through my life.

Maybe tonight, if it doesn't rain, I'll go look at the moon from the beach — how long since I've done that and think about You.

Whom I love above all.

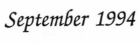
September 1994

September 2, 1994 — Grand Beach, Michigan

My Love,

Happiness, Red Warren tells me this morning in his poem "Last Walk of the Season," has no measurable pace and hence one must not count years, one must not ask, he says, whether this walk with his wife will be the last time he will ever take the walk.

Happiness is to be reveled in while it exists without any thought of what comes next. The last weekend at Grand Beach must be enjoyed for itself regardless of the fact that the weeks and months ahead look pretty grim.

I will try to follow that advice this weekend and enjoy it all as a sign of Your love. No, more than that, as a sacrament of Your loving presence among us.

I love You.

September 6, 1994 — Grand Beach, Michigan

My Love,

Red Warren's poem this morning is about looking at his baby picture with his parents in the picture. He laments the death of his parents as they lie side by side in whatever love survives under the grass or snow. He hopes that perhaps their love lasts somewhere else. Then he turns to himself as "he in guilt grieves/over nameless promises unkempt, in undefinable despair."

Yi!

Some of that may be his rock-ribbed Baptist guilt, some of it free- floating guilt, but much of it I recognize, the guilt over so much not done, so many opportunities missed, so much wasted effort, so much misspent energy, so much love ruined, so much unnecessary angry feeling, so much of an inadequate life.

If this year of my journal ever becomes public, people may laugh that I should feel that way after all I have done. But Warren felt that way and he did a lot more than I have. One feels sadness and guilt not in comparison with others but in comparison with one's own dreams and hopes and promises.

I am sorry for the mess I have made of my life. Help me to do better in whatever years (or months or weeks) You have allowed me. I love You.

September 11, 1994 — Grand Beach, Michigan

My Love,

Last day at Grand Beach. Almost packed. Thanks for the graces of the summer. I need a vacation!

Sorry I messed up so badly. I love You.

September 12, 1994 — Chicago

My Love,

The Arts & Entertainment people are here to interview me for their documentary about Santa Claus, which is of course about You and Your love for all of us as Your children. A beautiful story and one that is True even if it is not literally true....

A couple of hours later now. A & E has left. It went well enough. How could one miss on Santa Claus?

Yet I feel a little hypocritical. I spoke of wonder and surprise but there I am with much of the capacity for wonder and surprise drained out of my life.

Not all and not permanently, not at any rate with the help of Your grace.

So I beg You to help me, to return to my ability to be astonished.

I love You.

September 13, 1994 — Chicago

My Love,

I didn't sleep much last night. I was up at 4:30 after maybe two hours sleep. Transition trauma, getting ready for the trip, major crisis in a family to whom I'm close — unwed teenage pregnancy. Tough, brave young woman. Immediate family is acting right though under strain. More distant family pushing for abortion. I called the young woman and said that if I wasn't asked to baptize the child I'd disown the lot of them and congratulated her. Such kids who reject the easy way out are brave, brave women and should be praised. She'll be an even stronger person because of it. I pray for her and all her family and for the child.

I'm sure You're proud of her too.

I love You.

Help me to love You more.

September 17, 1994 — Chicago

My Love,

My father died forty-seven years ago today. All the images come flooding back, being pulled out of line coming out of chapel, the train ride in, taking a taxi to the hospital, seeing his body unconscious from the stroke, the agony of waiting for him to die, the panic of the next several days, the terrible feeling in my stomach, the ache of returning to the seminary. All long forgotten consciously but still lurking in my unconscious and my dreams. I did not know him, not well, poor man, done in by the Depression. I respected him and indeed adored him, but I did not understand him. I'll be looking forward to meeting in the world to come.

Back to Christ the King today for the all-alumni reunion. I dreamed about going back there last night. How often I have that dream. Were those the happiest years of my life? How can one answer that question? They were exciting, turbulent, hopeful years, years that shaped much of the rest of my life. It will always be my parish and my neighborhood.

I love You. Help me in this time of darkness to find the light.

September 15, 1994 — Grand Beach, Michigan

My Love,

The dentist managed to fix things in my mouth so that the fever is gone and the splint doesn't hurt any more and I can make the trip to Ireland. For which many thanks.

I don't like what I see in myself these days. My spirituality seems to have dried up and my faith, well, my faith seems inoperative. Maybe just being away from America and the phone, fax, and mail will be a good thing, a spiritual revival of a sort. Grant that I do not mess up too badly in my talk at Notre Dame tonight.

I love You. Help me out of this slump.

September 20, 1994 — Dublin

My Love,

The sun greeted me when I woke up after a good night's sleep, took one look at Dublin, and went and hid behind the clouds. But it's warm and not raining and I seem to be recovering moderately well from the jet lag. I like it here as much because it is peaceful for me as compared to Chicago as because it is a fascinating little country which is filled with surprises and about which I can always learn something new. How fortunate I am to be able to spend some time here, to become familiar with its customs and culture and people and understand myself in the process. To paraphrase Shaw, the Irish and the Irish Americans are two peoples separated by a common culture. The problem is that both are unaware that there is a common culture.

Despite the jet lag and the grim skies I'm more relaxed here than I was back home. Away from the fax and the phone and the mail. I need more time like that, and when I get home I will take steps to get it.

Thank You again for the trip. I love You.

September 22, 1994 — Dublin

My Love,

I'm on the train in the Heuston Station getting ready to leave for Galway to do research for my novel about the Tobias story, set in Galway City instead of Ectbana in Syria. Yesterday was a gorgeous day as today is predicted to be.

Conor and I started out to visit the new County Finngal, his home area, which I had never seen before and which is a charming place. But the weather was so fine that we decided to try for New Grange as the giant "passage tomb" is mistakenly called. Our neolithic ancestors surely knew how to build such tombs, which were in effect cathedrals for their culture and community. It was a brilliant stroke on their part to have the sun illumine the burial chamber on the day of the winter solstice — the sun's return promising the triumph of life over death, a celebration we continue at Christmas even today.

I found myself thinking about those people. We know practically nothing about them save that they were farmers and engineers and astronomers of considerable skill — and that they probably lived half the number of years that we do. Yet, if they weren't the very first Irish, surely some of their genes are in us. More to the point, they lived and loved and suffered and died just as we do and also hoped that death was not the end even as we hope. We live a lot longer than they did and can do a lot more things than they could do (like operate a subnotebook computer on a moving train!) but as to the meaning of human life and the significance of human love we are no farther advanced than they. We hope that death is not the end and that love is a hint of what comes next, just as they must have hoped.

In some matters there is no progress because there can be no progress.

But there is progress in Your self-revelation. Perhaps we know a little better who You are and hence have more grounds for hope. In Jesus You confirmed that indeed You are love.

So I try to love You and to commit myself again to You as I ride "into the west," tir-a-nog, the land of dreams and visions.

Weather permitting I'll fly out to the Aran Islands tomorrow. The next parish is on Long Island!

I love You.

September 24, 1994 — Dublin

My Love,

A fax from Chicago arrived under my door last night TV interview about how the Catholic Church will have to change to survive. Nonsense! It will survive whether it changes or not. Moreover I am fed up with interviews in which I must face stupid questions from ill-informed interviewers. And I don't like being harassed while I'm away. After I got here last night, *Time* was on the phone with questions about the Pope's accomplishments now that his health is in decline. I am tired of being the unofficial spokesman, the only priest from whom journalists can get the truth. It finally doesn't do any good for anyone.

There was a front-page story in the *Herald Tribune* this morning about the Pope's health and conclave rumors. Stupid story. Cited [Cardinal] Martini as the only candidate (there don't seem to be any other reasonable ones), then added that the Opus Dei would be against him. (It sure will.) It also said that the one who enters the conclave as *papabile* usually comes out still a Cardinal. Pacelli? Montini? Luciani? How dumb can a journalist be?

The issue is how independent can a local bishop be? Even conservative Cardinals want more independence. So the forces for moderate change have a chance, if only a slim one.

I conclude that papal elections may not be as important as they seem to be. It helps to have a good Pope, as Pope John demonstrated. But dependency on the papacy for change and growth may not be such a good idea. Bureaucrats usually respond instead of leading.

Yet I do hope and pray that someone like Martini is the next Pope. It will make things easier for everyone — Yourself included!

I love You.

September 26, 1994 — Dublin

My Love,

How quickly this week has slipped away. Tomorrow I go home with mixed emotions. I'm a little weary of living out of a suitcase, but I dread the exhaustion of the flight home and of the mounds of work that have piled up for me and the difficult two months ahead. I also find myself wondering as I always do why, given the fact I travel so badly, that I travel so much.

I watched part of the most recent film version of *Kim* yesterday afternoon. What a great story it is. I didn't catch the credits but the Holy Man had to be Sir Alec. Marvelous. But it made me realize that I am not a holy man, despite all my years of trying and despite the fact that ex officio I should be a holy man. I am not a man of prayer, nor a mystic, nor a contemplative. And if I've grown in the spiritual life since my days in the seminary, I hardly notice the results.

I understand that You love me regardless and that effort is what counts and not outcome. Yet I'm not even sure that my effort is all that strong or that pure. If I were a holy person perhaps I would not be so discouraged or weary or hassled as I am, nor would I be subject to interludes of rage and depression. Nor would I, perhaps, try to do so much.

Yet all of these things are hard to sort out. I work at being a good priest in the world in which I move, and at least sometimes succeed. I treat women with respect and a sense of equality, though that's no great achievement since that was the way I was raised.

So I find myself asking today if this whole week was not a waste of time and if indeed my whole life has not been a waste of time — and that despite the enthusiasm and respect of the priests with whom I met last night.

Anyway, thanks again for the trip and its graces, and please take care of me on the way home.

I love You.

Twelve hours from Chicago — if I'm lucky and there are no delays. This is the one bad part of the trip, getting from Dublin to Manchester and going through all the idiocy to check in for the flight to Chicago. Four-hour ordeal. As usual at this part of the trip I wonder why I came and why I'm here. It all seems a terrible waste of time.

I saw Brien Friel's new play *Molly Sweeney* last night. The difference between a great writer and a mere story teller. Why compare yourself to the best Irish playwright of the twentieth century? Why indeed?

His theme is that fact and fiction and fantasy are all ways of knowing. Molly loses both her new vision and her old vision but still *sees* more than she ever has. Wondrous. Right now I don't think I see anything.

She reminds me of a young woman dying at Billings hospital thirty years ago. She accepted her death but worried about her children and how they would remember her. Poor dear woman. I think I did all right in responding to her, though I don't remember what I said. I wanted to say more but before I could get back to the hospital again, she was gone, presumably dead. But then maybe in Your goodness not — though I don't see how she could have lived. I wanted to say more to her. I still want to say more. This time I would say it more easily, so perhaps I have learned a little something, though one can never be sure.

I know You took good care of her as You take good care of all of us. I love You.

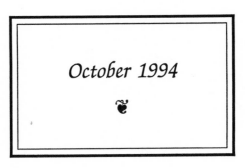

October 1994

October 3, 1994 — Chicago

My Love,

This morning Red Warren describes standing on a cliff above the ocean and pondering what it would be like to throw himself into it. He is not considering suicide. He was far too tough a redneck to think of that. He is merely contemplating the immensity of the sea and his own tininess in comparison.

The poem recalls something of my feelings as I walked along the lake front to and from the Bears game yesterday. Not that I even went as far as he did about throwing himself in. The lake looked far too cold even to think of that. But the vastness and the power of the lake is in a minor way a reflection of Your power, as tiny as it is in comparison with Your cosmos. Yet the lake can't think or love like I can (and You can). In that power to know and love and to yearn for the infinite and the ultimate, I continue to be fragile and ephemeral. Yet also to have an ability that the whole cosmos lacks. All the fire and movement and explosions in the cosmos do not reveal knowledge and love, yet I know them both. The expanding galaxies can't know You. But I can. They can't consciously be aware of Your love,

197

much less return it. But I can do both, however weakly and imperfectly.

For these graces I am grateful and I beg of You to grant that I use them well.

And I love You.

October 9, 1994 — Chicago

My Love,

I bet I'm the first one to be praying to You on a computer in the lobby of the Chicago Yacht Club! I drove in from Grand Beach this morning and got in a little early despite a flat tire on the skyway (city nail, the man who changed it said. I'll sue the mayor!). And I'm waiting for Dempsey to show up for our brunch before the Bears game.

It's a glorious day; the colors are changing, but the grass is still green and the lake is very blue, as is the sky. One more hint of You.

I must search for sacraments of You everywhere if I expect to hear You when You speak. I confess that I feel very much a failure this morning as both a priest and a Christian, both in the effects of my work and in my own personal life. But You still love me and Your love does not diminish because of my inadequacies.

Does anyone who is honest with himself/herself not feel a failure at the tag end of life? There were so many opportunities! Sure I took some of them, but how many of them have I wasted!

I'm glad I took the opportunity of these last three nights at Grand Beach. They were a wonderful rejuvenation, even if the effect will wear off soon. Thank You for that chance and all the graces You have bestowed on me during my life. I love You.

October 13, 1994 — Chicago

My Love,

A day off! How wonderful!

As I watched *All That Jazz* again yesterday I realized what an impact it has had on my images of You. Yet the film also renewed my image of You as a passionate and "uncanny" lover — aroused, determined, demanding, and frightening. It will be interesting to see what the students think about it next week.

I think I often don't accept the power of the metaphor of You as a womanly lover whom I need and who needs me. It is a shocking image, I suppose. While I accept it and teach it, I still do not ordinarily live as though it were less than the full truth about Your (demanding) passion. The scene in the movie in which Joe is about to die and the Angel of Death begins to undress so as to receive him on h(H)er marriage bed, so deftly done that I caught it only yesterday for the first time, is about as powerful an image of You as I can imagine. Yet who can deny it's truth — even if it is an image that would shock the various churches.

That I am vulnerable to You is acceptable. That You are hungry for me is too much. I usually refer to it — citing Exodus — as a sexually aroused groom hungry for his bride. But it is equally accurate and even more powerful to think of You as a sexually aroused bride eager for her groom.

A metaphor to be used sparingly, I think. But still to be used.

Help me to permit the metaphor to envelop and capture me.

I love You.

October 18, 1994 — Chicago

My Love,

The poem by Red Warren that I am reading today is about running down a beach to the point of exhaustion as a young man, seeking to find an experience that will convince his heart that there is purpose and meaning in life, a search he admits he will continue later in life.

Are such experiences possible? And do they finally really convince anyone? I know people who have had them who still act as if they believe in nothing at all, however conventionally religious they might be. Is it asking too much of You to expect such "heart-shattering" experiences of Your presence and Your love? It seems to be too much because most of us don't have them. If we did, faith might not be required and clearly part of the agony of our lives is the demand for faith. To be fully human, it appears, we must have some kind of fundamental trust in goodness — Goodness, whatever.

Moreover You could have replied to Warren that he already had confirmation in all the creatures about whom he made metaphors, that You spoke to him through creation. As You speak to me, through the loveliness of this Indian summer, through the charm of Stravinksy's *A Rake's Progress*, which we saw last night. If such diverse and utterly gratuitous glories do not convince me that there is purpose in creation, what can?

There is chaos too, of course. But chaos is what we would expect. It's beauty that comes as a surprise.

So I thank You for all the beauty and all the wonder and all the surprise — and also for our finally getting the books needed for the tour, to which I look forward with dread.

I love You.

October 20, 1994 — Chicago

My Love,

The promotion tour for *Irish Gold* promises to be a disaster. I must be patient in this mess. There is no point in being personally depressed about it, even if the aggravation is terrible. Help me to be patient and good-humored.

In his poem this morning Warren longs for a vision that would give meaning and purpose to his life. Then he concludes with two sad lines, "can it be that the vision has, long back, already come / and you just didn't recognize it?"

What a bleak possibility! You send Your visions all the time, I believe. If we don't recognize one, then there will be others. I have certainly seen You often in the objects and persons and events of my life. Though perhaps I am not so different from Red Warren. He looked for an extraordinary event (though he admits he might have missed it). I don't look for such events, but I am not as deeply influenced by the ordinary events as I might be or should be.

I should consider the possibility that a day like this and a month like the next month are an opportunity to find You even in the more difficult interludes of life.

I love You.

October 21, 1994 — Chicago

My Love,

Busy day, hour radio interview in the morning, finish up the Boston paper this afternoon. Book reading and signing at Waterstone's, then NORC trustees dinner. No time. Running. Discouraged about the book. But feeling good all in all. Great Indian summer weather continues.

I love You.

October 25, 1994 — Chicago

My Love,

I saw Giordano's *Fedora* last night, so-called *verismo* opera. Not what we would call realism today by any means but a tightly knit story of the sort that Puchini and other Italian composers turned to at the end of the last century. Very nice music with Dominio and Freni singing the leads. Sensational. Another grace, something lovely in the world that didn't have to be there.

Today in St. Mark I read the story about the calling of Levi and Jesus eating (at Levi's house) with tax collectors and sinners. The "kingdom" viewed from reading St. Mark like I had never read him before continues to be exciting: Your love sweeping into the world and embracing everyone, despite the displeasure of religious hypocrites. And He meant everyone, especially those who needed Him the most.

The hypocrites are still with us, and they still don't understand. Jesus ate with sinners, but today's scribes and Pharisees won't let those who are presumed to be in sinful marriages receive the Eucharist, which is patently a meal with Jesus. People exist for the sacraments and not vice versa. We have made so little progress and have learned so little. Fortunately many priests reject this moralism and realize that Jesus wishes to eat with sinners too.

In the poem this morning Red Warren recalls more images from his youth, this one fleeing from a revivalist camp meeting. According to an article in today's science section of the *New York Times*, vivid memories are stored in a special section of the brain. Maybe a good poet (or story teller) has a larger section for such memories. Heaven knows my imagination is flooded with such memories. A lot of stories still to write. One must listen to the grace in memory as well as to the grace in opera music.

The other day on the elevator I was standing next to a man who smelled of cigarette smoke, an aroma I usually, as You well know, abhor.

But this aroma was different, I know not why. It was pleasant and benign, because it reminded me of my father. What a wonderful image of grace in an unlikely place. I hope to see him again in Your world. I love You.

October 30, 1994 — NYC

My Love,

I thought I had packed my St. Mark commentary, but I guess I left without it. I can't even find a Gideon Bible in this room.

Despite a nap this afternoon and a good night's sleep last night, I'm still tired. I hope I'm not getting sick.

My paper was well received at the CCICA [Catholic Commission on Intellectual and Cultural Affairs] yesterday, by the young as well as the old. Thank You.

Take care of me on this trip and don't let me lose my temper. I love You.

October 31, 1994 — All Hallows Eve, NYC

My Love,

A wonderful Indian summer Halloween here in NYC. Temperature must be in the high seventies. No need for a coat or a raincoat.

The interviews are going well, though maybe I've "lost a step." I'm not quite as excited as I used to be. Or maybe not as quick (which would please June Rassner, who thinks I talk too fast) or maybe not as hopeful about this tour.

I am still on the clouds because of the kind woman at Waterstone's. Again many thanks for it.

And indeed for the many wonderful tricks and treats in my life.

Continue, please, to take care of me on this trip.

I love You.

November 2, 1994 — Washington, D.C.

My Love,

Wednesday night in Washington. Two incredibly busy days since I last entered a reflection. I am truly tired. I love You.

November 3, 1994 — Washington, D.C.

My Love,

I found a Gideon Bible at last and can continue my reflections on St. Mark. Strange translation. King James. The excitement continues. Jesus works miracles, cures the sick, casts out demons. Crowds flock to him. He slips away, perhaps because He doesn't trust the crowds. But the emphasis is on the excitement, the astonishment, the exhilaration of the Galilean new beginnings. Why does such excitement decline? I have asked that question often during these days. Now I remember the old saying that even revolutionaries have to sleep — probably because I need sleep so badly these days on the tour.

That's a concrete way of saying that we are limited by the weaknesses of human nature. We need to eat, we need to sleep, we need to take care of our families. All enthusiasms must wane somewhat. The secret is to be able to renew. Oh, how the Church needs renewal.

So do I. I must take time off this weekend.

I love You.

November 9, 1994 — Chicago

My Love,

The GOP won control of Congress yesterday, which is not a good thing for the Republic, though the Dems probably brought it on themselves. Poor Clinton, the most successful president in decades and people hate him. Still I bet that this defeat will be one more of those turnarounds in his life. I hope so.

I'm off on the tour again after class today. Not eager to do so. Nonetheless, the book is doing very well indeed, better than we had reason to hope. The title perhaps is the reason.

In today's reading from St. Mark we hear the parable of the seeds (as my commentator rightly calls it). It is one of the parables of reassurance — Your word and Your work will ultimately triumph, no matter how many setbacks. The early Christians needed to hear that both because of their own troubles and because at this point in the Gospel the enthusiasm and exhilaration of the story is breaking against the stone wall of suspicion, indifference, and skepticism. Yet Your son says that You will eventually triumph.

I believe this to be the truth. I need to keep the parable of the seeds in mind as I fly around the country.

I love You.

November 13, 1994 — Chicago

My Love,

Your grace is everywhere, as Red Warren reminds us in his poem about sunset today. I am running too rapidly to notice it. Help me, I beg You.

My notebook computer is still sick and the new one was sent by slow freight instead of fast. Dummies!

I have not lost my temper, though I have been close to it. Help me not to during the next few days.

I love You. Help me to love You more.

November 19, 1994 — Chicago

My Love,

The morning interview on WBEZ with Maura Tapp went very well. She had read the book, understood the story, liked the characters, and discussed the novel intelligently. But later in the day on the Chicago News TV I encountered just the opposite, an aggressively hostile interviewer who had read nothing but attacked me for what she had "heard" about my status in the priesthood and about my books. I tried to fight back but she wouldn't let me talk. Fortunately for me at the end of the broadcast two women called in to defend my books; not sexy stories, one of them said, but love stories. You have some fans out there, the announcer murmured. Yeah, I replied, people who have read my books.

I didn't read them, she said, but I talked to someone who had. So much for journalistic ethics. Donahue at least would have had enough sense to lie and claim to have read the books.

I calmed down eventually and thought of St. Mark and what happened to the parables. But even this morning I

am furious about the myth and my inability to counter it.
I suppose it will stick with me as long as I live and even
after I'm dead. Such is the price of trying something new.

An inkblot and a pin cushion for sickies.

June Rosner said I won going away in the discussion,
but I didn't feel that way. She also thought I reacted
appropriately, though I felt I was too angry.

I'll never win this one, and I ought not to let it disturb
my peace.

I love You.

November 22, 1994 — Chicago

My Love,

Very tired now. This is the first free moment all day. I
am very testy because of weariness and frustration. Sorry.

I wrote my Christmas newsletter about Santa Claus today. I offer You that as my reflection and a sign of my love
for the generosity of Your gift-giving.

November 29, 1994 — Chicago

My Love,

Yesterday was the first Sunday in Advent, a time of
hope, as I told the congregation on Saturday. I put up my
Christmas decorations yesterday, a chore without much
joy or hope in it. As I did so I noticed how much "junk"
I have accumulated through the years in this apartment.
Most of the "junk" isn't junk at all, but gifts from others.
Four crib sets! I can't throw them away, but they con-
tribute to the general disorder in the apartment and my
sense that there never will be time to straighten it out and
that the mess will persist till the end of my life.

How can I throw out crib sets?

The sad truth is that for a long time there hasn't been much hope in my life, save in episodic interludes. I need to revive it, but I'm not sure that's so easily done, especially when the world continues to close in and make ever more demands.

The lights and the ornaments, the crib scenes and the Santa Clauses in which my apartment abounds, the piles of Christmas presents that I am going to give others — all these are a challenge to my general discouragement and weariness, my weary and aging heart, my sense of defeat and failure, none of which are likely to be transformed by the two plane trips I must make this week.

I'm sorry. I'm not an Advent person this morning. I can, however, at least try to be more of an Advent person as this season goes on. Please help me.

I love You.

November 30, 1994 — Chicago

My Love,

Bill Schumacher is dead. I mourn for him.

Bill was so gifted. So very gifted. He made his contribution and it was important and I think he was happy or at least satisfied. But he could have been so much more. So could we all. I don't know what to make of any of it.

But I do know one thing, my dear Love: right now I'm going to bed.

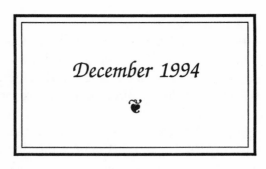

December 1994

December 1, 1994 — Chicago

I'm in the boarding lounge at Midway, waiting for South-west Airlines to carry me off to Louisville to talk at Hanover College. I wish I had time to learn more about the school before leaving. It was founded in 1827. Rush rush rush. But I slept for eleven hours last night, which was wonderful.

I still grieve for Bill Schumacher, which in part I realize is a grief for my own youth and for the frustrations and disappointments that have happened since then. But it is also grief for Bill personally, a brilliantly gifted man who died before his time and without his full talents ever being realized. Memories, good and bad, flood into my imagina-tion as I write these words. Grant him rest and peace and happiness. He is a child of Yours whom You love. Grant peace to all of us who were born and ordained in the old Church and who now serve with however much unease in the new.

I grieve for a generation. May our work and our dreams, our idealism and our disappointments, our com-promises and our loneliness all count for something in the plans of Your grace.

Thank You for the sleep. I love You.

December 2, 1994 — Chicago

My Love,

I continue to grieve for Bill. Roger Ebert's review of Krzysztof Kieslowski's film *Red* this morning was about gratuity, as is the film. People who do not have to meet but do. As I said to Roger in an E-mail message, the name of that is "grace" or "Grace," "Providence" or "providence." I don't know how You do these things but You do them and it is very clever of You, very clever indeed. I should stop trying to figure them out and simply accept Grace for what it is, Your ingenious love moving in incomprehensible ways in the world.

It was part of Your plan that I should know Bill and he should know me. We had only minor influence on each other's lives. Maybe we should have had more, though in truth, my Love, I think in the circumstances that was not the case. We knew each other, lived through seven years in the seminary together, then parted because of circumstances. Now he is dead, and I will be dead too before long. And Your grace continues to work.

What more than that can be said?

Anyway, I love You.

December 3, 1994 — Chicago

My Love,

A blessed Saturday off with nothing to do except read and relax. I'm going to try to read up on miracle in John Meier's new book about Your son. I am now in the midst of the first miracle section of Mark. Today I read the story of the calming of the waters. A lot of ink has been spilled about this and other miracles in recent decades, trying to explain them away. I think the major point to remember about this story, however, is that the apostles were terrified and Jesus was disappointed in them because they had not understood what he was about, did not realize that the kingdom was among them. Mark was aiming at the uncertainties of the community for which he was writing and for our uncertainties too. oh, we of little faith!

I really must straighten out my head on miracles, but that's not the point. I don't believe because of miracles. However, if there is an important point to the story in Mark, even those who had seen miracles experienced difficulty in believing, in permitting belief to light up their lives like a Christmas tree.

We are so worldly. I don't mean that we value the world too much (that might not be possible since it is a sacrament of You) but that we are so bogged down in work, fear, concern, obligations, and sheer bodily weakness and infirmity. The light of faith, the light of Christmas glows but dimly. Turn up the fire, if You please, and grant that faith in You and Your love may illumine my life so that my little faith grows a bit stronger.

I love You.

December 4, 1994 — Chicago

My Love,

I'm having supper with the Cardinal tonight. No major agenda, save some stuff about financial contributions. The much-heralded Lilly Endowment study of contributions comes up with exactly the same findings McManus and I reported seven years ago. Unless we deal the laity in as partners, there won't be a solution to the financial crisis.

I must run now to St. Mary of the Woods for Mass.

I love You.

December 5, 1994 — Chicago

My Love,

I read Mark's story of the exorcism in the Decapolis this morning. It continues the exciting story of the intervention of God in human history through Jesus who defeats evil wherever He encounters it. Perhaps the man was a manic depressive. I find that likely in the exorcism stories, but it doesn't really matter, does it? Indeed to cure a manic might just require more skills than to exorcise a demon.

Or maybe they come to the same thing. Father Meier argues that the miracles must be taken seriously because they are part of Jesus's persona whether modern rationalists like it or not. He also suggests that they are different kinds of miracles. I have no problem with the memory that Jesus worked wonders, because he surely did. That was part of the excitement of his mission. As to how to explain what mix of the natural and the supernatural, the explicable and the inexplicable constitutes the miracles, that is beyond our ability to sort out from the perspective of our time. If Jesus is who He seemed to think He was and if You are who You claim to be, then why hesitate about miracles, however hesitant one may be to accept a specific miracle claim? The universe is open, the world is wonder-full, and You are Love.

But what counts is power over evil, the evil of the sort I encounter in the books about war I've been reading the last few days.

Dinner with the Cardinal went well last night. His recent encounter with evil seems to have transformed him. He is particularly concerned now with liturgy and preaching. It will be interesting to see how the clergy react when they find out he is serious on these matters.

I love You. Help me to love You more.

December 6, 1994 — Chicago

My Love,

Back from Bill's funeral. Gray, foggy day. Depressing. St. Andrew's is an absolutely ugly church, vomity green paint, barrel wall. Yet the power of the liturgy and the power of faith, however weak it may be, broke through all the gloom. Bill is with You where some day, please You, we will all be. The tears have been wiped away as all our tears will.

My imagination was filled with pictures through the service, memories of the past. I lamented again that I had drifted away from the class and even from the archdiocese. It happened gradually and mostly unintentionally. I would have liked to have had more contact with Bill in this life. However, we both know, You and I, that my temptation to try to do everything is dangerous. I have done what I had to do and lost some other goods in the process. That is regrettable, and on a day like this it is sad, but it is also the way things are.

Fortunately it is not the way things are definitively. The muted joy of the liturgy, the sense of triumph of life over death means that there will be other times and other places and that nothing good or true or beautiful is ever lost.

The operative words on a day like this are St. Paul's (I think) "death shall have no power over us!" Right. Death does not end the possibilities. How they will be realized in the world to come we don't know, and it's up to You anyhow.

You usually do a pretty good job in such matters. So Bill and I will meet again.

I love You.

December 9, 1994 — Chicago

My Love,

Today is the feast of the Immaculate Conception, a feast of Your son's mother (who is a sacrament of You and who shapes much of my image of You). The doctrine is complex and confuses most people both in and out of the Church and presupposes a doctrine of original sin that needs rearticulation (though there certainly is something that answers nicely to the name of original sin operating in all of us). But it is easy enough to say that Mary was the most perfect woman, the most perfect totally human person who ever lived, and we know who and what she was from our knowledge of her son.

More to the point of that doctrine is the original story which is to be found in the Gospel, a story on which perhaps everything else is based, including Mary becoming the functional equivalent of a mother goddess (goddess of life) in the Catholic tradition. How fortunate we are to have a woman who reflects Your motherly and womanly love. It has made an enormous difference in my spiritual life, for which I am very grateful.

I must try to keep that image in my mind as I write my stories, always finding ways for it to illumine them so that, as Shags says, it will light up the rest of the story like a Christmas tree. I hunger to begin a new story, though in my schedule that will have to wait for spring.

Another busy day coming up, a long TV interview this morning.

I wonder why I bother with this stuff. In fact, however, having a priest on TV, a priest who is free to speak his own mind, is a good thing for the Church and for the tradition.

So I thank You for that too.

And I love You.

December 10, 1994 — Chicago

My Love,

In the passage from St. Mark today I read two miracle stories, that of the woman with the flow of blood and that of the twelve-year-old daughter of Jairus. They come from a pre-Marcan collection of miracle stories and in the context of his Gospel are part of the excitement and the energy of You entering human history in the person of Your son. Uncertainty about the miracle phenomenon should not distract us from the fact that times were changing dramatically when Your son began to preach. Now, all these years later, the excitement should still be there for those of us with faith, but alas, as I have often said, there is a tendency for the Good News to become Old Hat. All the talk from the Church about evangelization does not mean that Good News is in fact being preached. It's really just another form of triumphalism that makes religious leaders feel good, a buzz word devoid of meaning. When religious leaders show the same enthusiasm and excitement that St. Mark experienced, then talk about spreading the Good News will mean something.

Anyway, take care of me next week during the book promotion tour. Help me to do well and to radiate Your love.

I do love You.

December 11, 1994 — Chicago

My Love,

Jim O'Connor called yesterday to report another death in the class — Joe Hudik. A man of considerable talent, he has been burdened by poor health for at least twenty years. Grant him the fullness of eternal Happiness. Jim also went through a list of other classmates who are sick, most with some variety of lung disease that can be traced to smoking, which again can be traced to the idiotic smoking rules at the seminary, which made men chain smokers during the brief time they had to smoke each day.

Help them all. Help us all.

Jim said that some of the crowd were worrying, with characteristic Irish superstition, who the third one would be. A scary thought when I'm making a turn around the country on a promotion tour this coming week. In fact, I'll be safer in the planes than I would be on the Chicago expressway.

Of course, I don't want to die. No one does, not even Your son. But I asked myself yesterday what would be missed if I'm number three. It is a commentary on how little joy there has been in my life in recent years, that, while I certainly do not want to die, I wouldn't have all that many regrets. I certainly don't feel that I have unfinished work to do.

Which is not to say that there is not work still to be done. I'll try to do whatever must be done for as many years as You give me life. I'm merely saying that I feel a sense of completion at the present time, which doesn't necessarily mean that my life or work is complete.

In some sense my reaction is not a healthy one. Have I so completely lost my energy and enthusiasm and exuberance? I hope I am not becoming an embittered cynic. Yet there are times when I am dangerously close to that. I give a good imitation of a joyous person a lot of the time, and in fact I am some of the time, but there is still the underlying angst that comes, I suppose, from so many failures and so much wasted effort.

Well, I certainly have an agenda for my retreat next week. And a goal to be joyous and not merely appear so on this trip. I love You.

December 12, 1994 — Chicago

My Love,

The annual Christmas gathering of my friends from St. Angela last night was a wonderfully joyous and happy evening. The three married couples are clearly satisfied in their relationships, a satisfaction that like all marital successes must have been bought through much suffering and conflict and discouragement, but that now surely seems to them well worth all the effort. The final years of a marriage are obviously the best, especially if health survives. It is good of You to give people more time to enjoy those years.

What impresses me about these people is that they grew up as I did in the old Church and have adjusted enthusiastically to the new Church, more so perhaps than many priests of our generation. One couple had experimented with the Opus Dei for a year and got out because it wasn't their world, which ought to have been clear to the Opus people from the beginning. All the others had horror stories about priests that make me sick at heart. They know there are good priests too, but that does not undo the stupidity, the arrogance, the insensitivity, the cruelty of so many priests. It's a wonder we haven't driven them out of the Church. We sure as hell have tried.

But as Rita said, it's a gift, and no stupid priest is going to take that gift away. The others agreed.

The laity are the strength of the Church; the priests are the weakness. The laity have a far deeper spirituality than we have. If only we could be humble enough to learn from them.

I love You. Take good care of me on this crazy tour that begins tomorrow morning.

December 14, 1994 — En route from Houston to Minneapolis

My Love,

We're about forty-five minutes out of Minneapolis Metro and I am utterly exhausted. The reaction in Texas was very friendly. I had forgotten what a friendly state it is. The interviews went well, and I got a lot of opportunity to talk about *Irish Gold*. I continue to wonder whether all the travel and all the talk do any good at all. I'm on the trip because it might help and because the media are a necessary platform for the Church. But I'm skeptical about whether it's worth it all, but that might be because I'm so tired.

I left the cable for the battery home — I never remember to bring everything I should — and am on my second battery. So I must be limited in what I say.

I am more and more impressed by the religious faith of the lay people and secondarily about how my fiction sustains so many of them. I'm grateful for that, and I realize how important the books are and that I must continue to do a good job with them. For that I beg Your help.

Take care of me on the rest of this mad trip. And help me to be the kind of priest and the kind of person who illumines ever more the vision I try to preach.

I love You.

December 20, 1994 — Chicago

My Love,

I've been listening to Shea's tapes on the spiritual life. Very good, as one might have expected. They make me realize how impoverished my spiritual life is. I found myself thinking that I ought to retire to devote more of my time to You. Then I realize that's a cop-out. Jack says in effect the same thing on the tape. One is not supposed to cut everything or anything off. One must rather integrate. Even if I did retire, what would I retire from? And how would things be any different?

The problem is not in the environment. It's in me.

He had a nice story about a man who rode through many towns on an ox and told the folks he was looking for an ox. They laughed at him. Finally in one town, someone said, "You're crazy, holy man. You say you are looking for an ox, but you're already riding one."

"So it is with you and God," he replied. "You claim to be searching for Him but He is already with You."

So You're always with me. I know that, of course, but I don't always or even often pay attention. And when I am as tired as I am now (and as I usually seem to be), it's hard to be aware of anything more than the work that must be done and the sleep I need.

Was this promotion tour necessary? I think it was. But the question is how I stay in touch with You no matter how busy I am. That's an issue I hope to address in the days ahead.

I love You. Help me.

December 23, 1994 — Chicago

My Love,

It's now officially winter. Night not only for most of the day but dark even during the day, but mild, thank You. I'm off retreat and feeling somewhat better and at least more relaxed despite my stomach virus. I will attempt to radiate the Christmas joy on which I wanted to reflect but was unable to do so much because I was sick.

I will try again tomorrow on Christmas Eve to return to joy and the glory, the excitement and the hope of Christmas. Help me please.

I love You.

December 24, 1994 — Chicago

My Love,

Most of the stories in the book of Christmas stories I read during my ill-fated "retreat" were about lonely and isolated people at Christmastime. Only one of them really managed to reconnect, and he did it with regret. Thus the theme of modern literature, the isolate, the alienate as hero.

Yet there are many isolates out there in the world this weekend. I talked to one this morning (You know who it was), a person of enormous generosity and kindness. The person does not deserve to be alone but nonetheless is. I want to pray this morning for her and all those who are isolated or lonely at Christmastime, including those who are isolated or lonely even if they are surrounded by others.

How much loneliness there is in the world. How much isolation. Christmas of course does not cause it; it merely reveals it. Some are in the world of loneliness because of mistakes, some because of accidents, some because they choose it, some because for reasons of nature or nurture they have no choice. You love them all. I hope that Your love shines through on them during this joyous season.

I look back on all my Christmases. Some were good, some were not so good. None were bad because I did not rejoice in the season, though I do remember the bad times when I first moved in here that I didn't even have a Christmas tree. Fortunately that was only a brief time in my life. In the last twenty years or so they have been wonderful.

Thank You, by the way, for all the marvelous Christmas cards with the notes of appreciation on them for my work.

I wish to pray for the repose of the soul of Dan Herr today. My Christmas Eves with him were wonderful. I miss him still.

I have recovered completely from my virus, for which also many thanks. I won't be dragging tomorrow.

I love You. Help me to love You more.

December 25, 1994, Christmas — Chicago

My Love,

An incredibly lovely Christmas Day, clear sky, temp in the fifties. Wonderful and thank You.

The virus lingers. I wake up in the morning feeling good and then collapse about noon. Today I seem better. I hope so, as there is much to be done today.

I did manage to listen to more of Jack's tapes yesterday in what was a mostly unsuccessful attempt to salvage my retreat. The tapes were fine, and one of the blessings of the retreat is that I listened to them.

Today is what it is all about, the explosion of what Your son called the "kingdom" and what we might call "power," though we don't have a good word for it. Your lurking love, which beat at the heart of the universe, could no longer be contained, and it broke through at Christmas and then appeared dramatically during his public life, death, and resurrection.

Light came into the world, a light that had always been there but finally appeared with such incandescence that all must see it, a light that no one can ever put out — though we followers of the light oft-times dim it.

A light for which this bright Christmas day is a better metaphor than snow — safer too.

Help me to be cheerful as I pass through my various stops (*five*) this day and radiate the joy that the light requires and demands — even if I continue to feel poorly.

I should smile as I did on the Santa program, which I finally saw last night, a wild, mad-cap Irish smile, a smile for Santa and for Christmas.

Merry Christmas to all.

Jack says You live through us. I will reflect more on that tomorrow. Now it seems fitting to wish You a merry Christmas too, an exuberance of joy from the creatures You love, wafting up to heaven (You should excuse the metaphor) and filling You even more full than You are with our happiness.

I love You, light shining in the darkness.

December 25, 1994 — Chicago

My Love,

Christmas day winds down, a good Christmas day despite my virus (which lingers, though now only just barely). Maybe it was the weather, maybe it was the quiet during my retreat, maybe it was Jack's tapes, maybe it was the imagery of Christmas. Anyway it was a much better Christmas than most, and I come home tonight more relaxed, more happy, and more confident than I have been on many other Christmases. For this many, many thanks.

Even the Durkin party, which could have been so sad, was bright and upbeat with only a few appropriate tears when Eileen read her toast. Both she and Dan are natural poets; they have all the moves and the imagery. I hope they use their talent. There is nothing more destructive than unused talent. Talent, as I have said so often to members of my group in days past, is not an option, it is a demand. I hope Dan and Eileen gain the confidence necessary to use what You have given them.

The imagery might have had more of an impact on me if I were not partially ill and if my retreat was not such a bust, but even under such circumstances, even half a nod in the direction of the imagery transforms everything. Thank You for the day. Back to this subject tomorrow.

December 26, 1994 — Chicago

My Love,

Another glorious day in Chicago — temp to go to the high fifties. Christmas parties go on. Too much food.

If I try to recast Jack's spiritual theory, it emphasizes, as a Catholic should, Your immanence. You are present in us. Not only, as I so often say, lurking in the persons, objects, and events of life but also in the very self as a person and an event and as a subject. The spiritual life is less about breaking out of the self to build a bridge to You, and more about recognizing You present in the self, the Spirit talking to our spirit as St. Paul put it. There is nothing startling or especially new about such a presence. It is often called grace, isn't it? However, in theology Grace can be lost, but not grace, not Your presence, not Your love, not Your passion in living out Your life in our life. Hence I use the small letter, but I'm not so sure the two realities are all that different. Nothing can alienate You from us.

Building up a whole spirituality on Your presence, Your actual, vital dynamic presence is another matter altogether, though that's in the tradition too.

The sacraments all around us, natural and religious, ought to be not merely metaphors for Your presence in the world but also reminders of Your presence in the self.

In effect when I write these reflections I am not talking to Someone out there, but to Someone in here. You are there of course, but it is in that mysterious graceful union between You and me in the fine point of my soul that You hear my prayers.

I know that. I've known it all along. Yet after listening to Jack's tapes it is clearer to me than it ever was. I must try in the days and weeks and months ahead to listen carefully to You and to believe that You listen carefully to me.

I love You.

December 27, 1994 — Chicago

My Love,

Shea and I saw *Nell* last night. Super acting and some interesting commentary on human nature, not as anti-society as some of the critics claimed. However, any film that casts psychologists and the media as villains has a lot going for it. I viewed the story as a vindication of the dignity and resiliency of human nature. What strange creatures we are, capable of such extraordinary accomplishments and so many cruelties, of passionate dedication and of quick decline and death.

However, the light continues to shine in the darkness and the darkness will never put it out. You lurk everywhere, keeping the light bright and sustaining its glow. We find You in the other, but, I think, even more in our response to the other. We find the other appealing despite flaws, just as You find us appealing despite our flaws. So the other is God to us and reminds us of the God within us who loves the way we do — and loves the other too.

A very clever arrangement!

I love You.

December 29, 1994 — Chicago

My Love,

The cold continues, the one in my head that is. Outside the weather continues lovely with the rising sun illuming the city in Rembrandt colors. More than a week of sickness now. It's tiring, but there are worse sufferings that I have been spared. But I think I'm getting better, though I've thought that before.

The year winds down and I must recapitulate. First of all, the good things for which I am grateful.

Three trips to Europe, all of which were successful and none of which wearied me to much. Five books published, all of them it would seem successful. I think I've grown closer to You and understand You better. More support from friends and readers than ever before. Good health (which even the present minor sickness does not negate).

Failures: prayer life slips when I am stretched too far. Which this last year was a lot. Not much of a vacation in the summer. Both my fault. I'm sorry. Crazy hurried exits from my apartment. No constant sense of hope and love and faith. Too much work?

Loss: Jack Durkin. I regret that circumstances were such that I didn't know him better.

Worries: Still no new book contract. State of the Church.

Not a complete list. I'm still not up to par. More tomorrow.

I love You.

December 30, 1994 — Chicago

My Love,

Strange dream last night. I was running through the streets of Tucson with a group of young people (I was

young too!) trying to escape from adults, parents I presume. It was an imaginary Tucson like the complicated
imaginary Chicago my dreams have created — real street
names but unreal though elaborate neighborhoods. In one
part of the run I started dodging through homes, the doors
of all of which were open. A woman from one of the
houses began to chase me too. She was closer than the
other adults and fast. Somehow I managed to duck away
from her, though perhaps temporarily, and arrived at the
bus station where the finale was to be enacted. But I woke
up. A very vivid dream that continued each time I woke
and went back to sleep. The leader of those chasing me
seemed to be my neighbor Cal Potts, one of the world's
true gentle men.

I suspect that I am thinking more of Tucson as a place
to relax, like I think of it every year whatever the reality
turns out to be and am running from those who want to
consume my time and take away my freedom.

I must resist that pressure this year. I must not let my
afternoons be take away. Even if it means turning off the
phone. It is not a vacation. There are things to be done and
things I will do, but I will not, cannot, should not run the
way I did this last quarter. No way. Help me to really mean
it this time.

Thank You for the extra special gifts, one in particular
of this year.

I do not ask that I escape running. I ask rather that I
run effectively.

I love You.